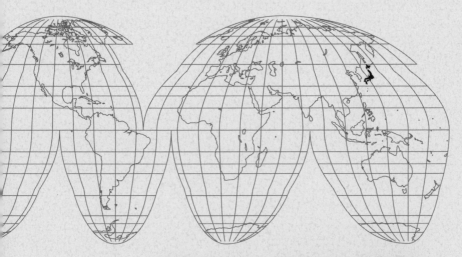

GLOBAL CLASS JAPANESE SMEs

JAPAN LIBRARY

GLOBAL CLASS JAPANESE SMEs

Makoto Kurosaki

Translated by Larry Greenberg

Japan Publishing Industry Foundation for Culture

Translation Note

Japanese terms, including the names of persons and places, are in principle romanized according to the Hepburn system, with the exception that no distinction is made between short and long vowels. The names of Japanese persons are written in English word order, with the given name preceding the family name, e.g., Tozaburo Hasegawa.

Global Class Japanese SMEs
by Makoto Kurosaki. Translated by Larry Greenberg.

Published by
Japan Publishing Industry Foundation for Culture (JPIC)
3-12-3 Kanda-Jinbocho, Chiyoda-ku, Tokyo 101-0051, Japan

First edition: March 2017

Originally published in Japanese language as *Sekai ni kantaru chusho kigyo* by Kodansha Ltd. in 2015.

English publishing rights arranged with Kodansha Ltd., Tokyo.

Jacket and cover design by Kazuhiko Miki, Ampersand Works
Front jacket and cover photos:
Upper left: Spring (Tokaibane Mfg. Co., Ltd.), Center left: Mechanical switch for setting precise locations (Metrol Co., Ltd.), Lower left: Preserved flowers (OHCHI NURSERY LTD.), Center: Scissors (TOKOSHA CO., LTD.), Upper right: Capsule endoscope, Sayaka (RF Co., Ltd.), Lower right: Large slewing bearings (ANTEX CORPORATION)

As this book is published primarily to be donated to overseas universities, research institutions, public libraries and other organizations, commercial publication rights are available. For all enquiries regarding those rights, please contact the publisher of the English edition at the following address: japanlibrary@jpic.or.jp

Printed in Japan
ISBN 978-4-916055-81-1
http://www.jpic.or.jp/japanlibrary/

CONTENTS

Preface for the English Edition —— 5

Introduction —— 7

Chapter 1
World Leaders Employing Traditional Technologies
Five Companies – "We're Not Trying to Be Toyota" —— 13

Chapter 2
Specialization is the Key to Success
A Look at Five Companies:
"We Won't Go as Far as Discounting Prices Just to Make a Sale" —— 47

Chapter 3
Four Companies Taking on the World with Highly-Advanced Technologies
Undaunted by Domestic Harassment —— 81

Chapter 4
Controlling Niche Markets Inaccessible to Big Firms
Six Companies – "No Need for an Administrative Department" —— 107

Chapter 5
Winning with "Business Category Changes" that Capitalize on Expertise
Four Companies, Including One that
"Will Not Move the Operational Core to China" —— 141

References —— 167

Preface for the English Edition

I wrote this book to tell readers about the business know-how of small- and medium-sized enterprises (SMEs) in Japan and how they have developed their technologies. The companies I chose to cover occupy niche markets, but some are doing things that nobody else in the world is. Others may not be so unique, but they have an overwhelming share of the global market. Some, wielding advanced technologies that no other company on Earth can imitate, are at the very top of their fields, not only in Japan but across the world.

There are 3.85 million SMEs in Japan. To be honest, 1,000 or more of these businesses fit the description in the preceding paragraph, although even Japan's Ministry of Economy, Trade and Industry is not entirely sure of the precise number and there must be, at the very least, tens of thousands of other companies that are near their level.

It used to be that Japanese industry produced goods of such low quality that the country's products were synonymous with being cheap and shoddy. Today, however, the world respects Japanese products for being safe and high in quality. Chief examples include automobiles, robots and the Shinkansen bullet trains. An automobile is assembled from over 20,000 parts and most of them are made by SMEs. Japanese cars have a solid reputation for being fuel-efficient, reliable and safe because they are built with fine components manufactured by SMEs. Toyota's renowned Just-in-time (JIT) production system has been introduced in numerous production sites across the globe. It involves delivering to assembly plants parts in only the quantity they are needed, when they are needed, and these parts are built to meet specifications down to the nanometer.

The underlying strength of SMEs supports the Toyota JIT production system. The Japanese Shinkansen high-speed trains race along at speeds of over 300 km/h while traveling only a few minutes apart from each other. Japan is an earthquake-prone country that has been rocked by many a mighty earthquake, while several large typhoons hit the archipelago every year. And yet, the Shinkansen has been in operation for over 50 years and has never once experienced a major accident. Parts produced by many SMEs are used to build the Shinkansen's safety features, carriages, bodies and rails. The Shinkansen's reputation for safety has been maintained by the excellent components these SMEs make. And in many other fields, components built by SMEs play a crucial role in equipment, devices, robots and other creations designed to maintain some of the best living conditions in the world here in Japan.

In addition to advanced countries like the United States and those in Europe, many developing countries in Asia—as well as China, which continues to post annual growth rates of 6% as its economy has rapidly expanded for over a decade—have come out with policies to foster the growth of SMEs. It is a sign that helping such enterprises grow has become a global issue. For a long time, many countries worked very hard to build up large companies occupying a central place in their industries. It is the opposite today, as there has been a major shift to supporting SMEs as the seeds of industry. And although there is a worldwide effort to help SMEs grow, the policies of national governments alone are insufficient to accomplish this goal. That is because much of it hinges on how the enterprise is managed, the passion that entrepreneurs have for their business, as well as their competency.

This book goes into great detail on such matters as the passion of entrepreneurs and how they have sharpened their skills. I firmly believe that this text will prove truly useful for SME managers and employees around the world, as well as for policymakers tasked with helping these businesses succeed.

Professor Makoto Kurosaki
Faculty of Economics
Teikyo University
November 2016

Introduction

My greatest incentive for writing this book is my belief that Japanese manufacturing and the resurgence of the small to medium-sized enterprises (SMEs) that undergird the industry will revitalize the Japanese economy. In World War II, Japan lost approximately 25% of its national wealth, such as railroads and ships. It is said that between 2.55 million and 3 million Japanese were killed or missing in action. At the war's close, the Japanese economy was beset by severe inflation and food shortages. The country hit rock bottom in the conflict's immediate aftermath, as its citizens were supplied with only small quantities of rations and 10 million people feared they would starve to death. Thereafter, however, the Japanese economy recovered and by the 1960s posted a high annual growth rate of 10%. In 1968, Japan overtook West Germany to become the world's number-two economy.

Japan's reign as the second-largest economy on the planet lasted for 42 years, until China took over that distinction in 2010. Although second place has been handed over to China, Japan is still our world's third-largest economic power. Japan, which has few natural resources within its borders, such as iron ore, petroleum and coal, has retained its economic standing thanks to an economy structured to trade in added value: the country imports resources, which are processed into products for export. Japan's value of exports in 1960 was 1.45 trillion yen, but this rose to 6.95 trillion yen in 1970. That is an increase of 370% in only a decade. Export value continued to grow another 320% in the 1970s. These statistics clearly demonstrate that it was as a trading nation that Japan achieved rapid growth.

If we exclude the shipbuilding industry, the mainstay of these exports were textiles, toys and light machinery manufactured by SMEs. The focus of Japanese exports eventually transitioned to the heavy and chemical industries, as exemplified by railways and chemicals, and then to televisions and other home appliances. The great transformation has since progressed further, represented by advanced industries exporting products like semiconductors and automobiles. In the meantime, Japan's international competitiveness has become so strong that many times the country has experienced friction over trade with America. Although Japanese goods used to be synonymous with being cheap and shoddy, in the 1980s that reputation took a U-turn as Japanese products came to be known as affordable, safe and high in quality.

However, when the bubble in Japan's asset-inflated economic growth burst in the 1990s, there was nothing but bad news out of the nation's economy as it fell off a cliff.

Even so, a look at UN statistics on global GDP show that in 2000, at the turn of the century, while the United States accounted for 31%, Japan's GDP was roughly half that at 14.2%. To put it another way, the two countries of Japan and the United States represented nearly 50% of global GDP. Germany made up 5.9%, Britain 4.7% and France 4.1% of global GDP and the combined total of these three countries was comparable to Japan's GDP.

At present, though, Japan's share in this period of general global growth has fallen to between 8% and 9%. Japan enjoyed a trade surplus that was one of the largest in the world, but in 2011 that turned into a trade deficit. There was a time when approximately 80% of all flat screen televisions were made by Japan, but now that figure has dropped to between 10% and 20%. Likewise, while Japan reportedly used to manufacture half the world's semiconductors, that share too has fallen to between 10% and 20%. And in the shipbuilding industry, where people used to say Japanese industry had conquered the Seven Seas, South Korea and China, where wages are lower, have caught up and turned Japan's former glory into a faded memory.

Be that as it may, Japan is still one of the leading producers of automobiles and there is no doubt that there are many industries where Japan has a top share of the market, such as high-quality materials for advanced industries including robotics, carbon fibers and engineering plastics. In addition, nano-technology is gaining notice as a leading industry in the 21st century. In this field, manufacturers craft products with a precision of one-millionth of a millimeter and one-billionth of a gram. Japan is generally recognized as setting the highest standards for nano-technology. Further examples include physics, chemistry and medicine. The numerous Japanese winners of the Nobel Prize in Physiology or Medicine for their accomplishments in the field of natural science prove that Japan is a scientific and technological powerhouse. In other words, Japan is still leading the world in advanced and ultra-advanced industries. I believe that further enhancing the international competitiveness of these industries will lead to the rehabilitation of the Japanese economy.

Japan's advantage is the presence of numerous strong SMEs that support these advanced industries. According to *2014 White Paper on Small and Medium Enterprises in Japan*, there are 3.864 million companies in Japan, of which no more than 11,000 are large enterprises. In contrast, there are 3.853 million SMEs. That means 99.7% of all Japanese firms are SMEs. The number of people employed by each category of business is 13.97 million at large enterprises and 32.17 million at SMEs, which means that the latter accounts for 70% of employment. SMEs even outperform their larger counterparts in terms of the amount of added value: 147 trillion yen for SMEs and 125 trillion yen for large enterprises. Except for the turbulent period after World War II, Japan's SMEs have contributed a fairly steady ratio of around 55% of all added value, a proportion which they have continued to maintain. SMEs don't just support Japan—they form the core of the Japanese economy.

The important role that SMEs play was made most evident by the Great East Japan Earthquake. Many small businesses that manufacture parts out of local factories in the Tohoku and North Kanto regions suffered damage to their production facilities and were forced to shut down operations. A memory that is still fresh in my mind is that when these small factories stopped producing parts, they created serious problems for the manufacture of automobiles, which is one of Japan's leading industries. It is inarguable that many Japanese citizens had never imagined small local factories could be so vital as to bring manufacturing in a giant industry like automobiles to a halt.

Among those SMEs are many small businesses that have fully grasped the advanced engineering involved in nano-technology so they can make world-class products in their local factories. Additionally, there are many Japanese SMEs that have used their traditional yet masterful skills to create niche products that are wholly original and not to be found in any other company's lineup. You will discover detailed examples as you read this book, but I would like to mention here that Japan's cutting-edge automobile industry, the Hayabusa asteroid probe, the Shinkansen bullet trains, the linear motor used in maglev trains and the Tokyo Skytree, which is the tallest structure in Japan and the tallest tower in the world, are all symbols of Japan and all of them had many of their parts fabricated by SMEs. Moreover, in many cases Japanese SMEs play such a crucial role that the global economy would come to a standstill without their products.

According to the Japan Bank for International Cooperation (JBIC), the percentage of production that Japan's manufacturing industry performs outside the country reached 35.2% in the fiscal year beginning April 1, 2013, while the bank estimates this proportion will rise to 39.9% by fiscal 2017. Japanese companies began relocating their manufacturing centers overseas in the late 1980s and domestic industry has experienced a growing hollowing out ever since. Nobody has been hit harder by this trend than SME manufacturers, as their numbers have shrunk from 310,000 companies in 2000 to 189,000 firms as of 2012. That latest figure is a 60% drop from the peak of 438,000 enterprises in 1985. The reason behind this lies in their exposure to price competition from China and other developing countries where wages are extremely low.

There are still many SMEs that are hard at work. You can see them in local clusters of factories, bustling with the sounds of machinery and the voices of people at work. However, they have lost their former potency. If one examines Japan's SME policies back in the Meiji Period (1868-1912), one finds that Japan was ahead of the rest of the world. However, Western countries, particularly those in the EU, have always considered SMEs to be the seeds of economic growth and they have come out with economic policies founded in this belief and worked furiously to improve educational systems. More recently, China, South Korea, Southeast Asia and other parts of the world have adopted this approach as well. In contrast, Japanese SMEs currently find themselves in such severe circumstances that we could call it an ice age.

This book is the story of SMEs that have conquered the world despite this challenging situation. It is said that the Japanese economy shows some promise, while calls have been made for the revitalization of communities outside of Japan's major cities. But the rehabilitation of capable SMEs is an absolute requirement if we are to attempt to stimulate these local economies by having them ride on the coattails of Japan's economic recovery. For this reason it is my sincere hope that many people will be cheered by reading this book and that it will rally the spirits of SME managers, employees and students who aspire to work at one of these enterprises. It should also be noted that I have dispensed with honorifics in the text.

In researching this book I was able to speak directly with the top person at each company, whether a president or chairperson. Many of the businesses even gave me personal tours of factories and other production sites. They were also kind enough to give me thoroughly detailed explanations of terminology and other complicated matters. I would like to convey my gratitude to them here.

I also want to express my regrets to the companies I researched but whom I could not include due to the limited number of pages. The Small and Medium Enterprise Unit at the Japan Finance Corporation (JFC) was of tremendous assistance for introducing me to companies and acting as a go-between. I would also like to mention that the JFC was able to introduce me to such excellent enterprises because it has helped build up over 600 listed firms. I was also greatly aided by the plethora of advice and page layout help provided by Katsuya Maruyama, who works in the General Knowledge Books Department at Kodansha Ltd. I was only able to complete this book with the assistance of all these people. I would like to thank them once more.

Makoto Kurosaki
January 2015

Chapter 1

World Leaders Employing Traditional Technologies

Five Companies – "We're Not Trying to Be Toyota"

Chapter 1 introduces companies that have catapulted themselves to the top of the world by using technologies and techniques perfected in Japan. You can't really say that their industries are new and some of their industries are particularly Japanese. They are, however, fine examples that demonstrate how these industries and companies have become global leaders—if not the very best in the world—at what they do by combining the masterful skills they have built up in their long histories and traditions, with knowledge and innovation.

Too much *Kireaji* for the competition to catch up

As deflation has persisted in Japan, you can now go to a hardware store in the suburbs and find tools, like a pair of pliers or wire cutters, that are priced at only a few hundred yen. They even sell these things at the local 100 yen shop (the Japanese equivalent of a dollar store). Counterintuitively, this is also an era when high-priced pliers and wire cutters made by MARUTO HASEGAWA KOSAKUJO INC., based in Sanjo, Niigata Prefecture, sell for between 2,000 and 4,000 yen, which is equal to around 20 to 40 U.S. dollars. The company's high-performance plastic wire cutters, which are essential tools at production sites where workers manufacture items like mobile phones and advanced electronic devices, boast the largest market share not only in Japan but also in the United States. Maruto Hasegawa exports its products to over 20 countries around the world, but conducts nearly 100% of its transactions in Japanese yen so as to avoid risks associated with exchange rate fluctuations. Even so, production cannot keep up with demand, forcing the company to turn down some orders. This is a story that would make many small and medium-sized enterprises (SMEs) envious, but the secret is a *kireaji* (a Japanese word for "sharpness") that no other company in the world can imitate.

Keiba is the name of Maruto Hasegawa's brand of wire cutters and pliers. That brand name, as is the case with many Japanese SMEs enjoying great success in niche markets, is better known overseas than it is at home in Japan. That is because the people who work in the advanced manufacture of products like mobile phones and electronic devices that use plastic for raw materials or components are big fans of the brand. They say, "We wouldn't get anywhere with our work without Keiba wire cutters" and "Other companies' wire cutters quickly become dull." Maruto Hasegawa has been around for a good 90 years but the company's history has been one of coping with change and establishing a track record of improvement.

The city of Sanjo, where Maruto Hasegawa's headquarters and factory are located, has a long history of craftsmanship that goes back to the Paleolithic Period. During medieval times, makers of cast metal manufactured iron implements. Then, during the Edo Period (1603-1868), when the Tokugawa shoguns reigned over Japan,

Maruto Hasegawa wire cutters

Sanjo prospered as a city of artisans who primarily crafted carpenter's tools. Their wares ranged from kitchen knives and farm tools to *wakugi* nails made with original Japanese production techniques, as well as chisels, planers and files. Modern industry developed in the town during the Meiji Era (1868-1912). Lifestyles changed and smiths expanded into new fields while preserving and improving upon the traditions of their craftsmanship. The Shinto priests at Ise Shrine rebuild the structures there once every 20 years. At this time they carry out *shikinen sengu*, a regularly performed ceremony to relocate the enshrined deity. The 200,000 *wakugi* nails and 80,000 metal fittings used in the shrine rebuilding projects of 1993 and 2013 were supplied by the Sanjo Industrial Cooperative. This history and tradition of craftsmanship is alive and well at Maruto Hasegawa.

When Maruto Hasegawa was founded in 1924, the company started out making gluing clamps, a kind of carpentry tool. The switch from carpentry tools to other implements began when the business' founder, Tozaburo Hasegawa, began producing what was then a new kind of tool: pliers. He then purchased a spring hammer, a machine for shaping iron into instruments such as pliers. Tozaburo must have been highly determined, to have purchased a machine that was both modern for the time and expensive. Word that the company had begun using a large spring hammer spread not just in the thriving community of craftsmen in Niigata, but all across Japan. As a result, huge orders poured in from elsewhere in Niigata Prefecture as well as from Hokuriku, Osaka and elsewhere in the Kansai region of western Japan. And because Maruto Hasegawa was also improving on its technical competency, the company's tools established a reputation for reliability that was so good they were even used to repair warships. Tozaburo's ambitions had resulted in resounding success. The spring hammer that marked the turning point for the company is still today a respected symbol of progress and the bold determination to try new things and it graces the entrance to the head office.

Opening new sales channels

After the end of World War II, however, sales to the Japanese navy, which had been a major customer, evaporated. Japan's domestic manufacturing industry contracted during the turbulence of the postwar economy. Maruto Hasegawa made an all-out effort to market its wares to private Japanese enterprises, but the traditional manufacturers in Kansai were an impregnable stronghold that was not easy to break into. Despite a desperate, maximum effort to try and increase sales, it was largely unsuccessful. Tozaburo, the second-generation president of the company, who took over after his father, passed his days in constant worry. With doors blocking the company at every turn, Tozaburo received a suggestion from the president of a major tool wholesaler: "If it's so hard to sell here, then why don't you try overseas?" According to current company president Naoya Hasegawa, the truth may be a little bit different. "When I think about it now, it wasn't such a serious suggestion like 'why don't you start exporting?' Maybe it was something someone just said because (my father) was visibly troubled." In any case, Tozaburo, the second-generation president, jumped on the idea.

But it was unthinkable that a tool-making firm with nothing more than a small factory in Niigata would go up against the *shosha*, Japan's huge trading firms. So Maruto Hasegawa looked to the Japan Export Trade Promotion Agency, the predecessor to today's Japan External Trade Organization (JETRO). Japan at the time was suffering from massive trade deficit and was eager to boost exports as much as possible. This was also before the Joetsu Shinkansen bullet train line had been built, so even an express train took more than four hours to travel from Sanjo to Tokyo. Tozaburo, though, was adamant about making the trips to the Japanese capital, where he was introduced to big trading firms. He was also busy traveling to America in person to open up sales channels there. Tozaburo's successes included invitations to American buyers to visit the company's factory and show them how solid Maruto Hasegawa's technological capabilities were. He was also the beneficiary of fortunate timing.

The American economy was growing and its people were enjoying a plentiful consumer society. DIY shops (hardware stores) were opening up one after another from coast to coast and enjoying brisk sales of tools to a customer base that included do-it-yourself carpenters. Since buyers who had gotten a direct look at Maruto Hasegawa's production site knew just how good the tools were, sales steadily increased. Those sales, which at one point had amounted to only 100 million yen, rose to a peak of 1.7 billion yen, while annual production volume grew to 4 million units. However, the good times would not last forever.

Until then the yen-dollar exchange rate had been pegged at 360 yen to the dollar, but after the switch to a floating exchange rate system, the yen appreciated until the dollar was worth less than 300 yen. The value of the Japanese currency then continued to skyrocket to 200 yen to the dollar. Then came the decisive Plaza Accord of 1985. In a little over a year, Japan's currency appreciated from 230 yen to the dollar to 150 yen. Not only was this a major development affecting the survival of companies, but firms from countries like South Korea and Taiwan, where labor costs were cheaper, were improving their technical capabilities enough to make products rivaling those from Japan. Japanese exporters were hit with a double whammy as they increased prices to make up for the higher yen, but were embroiled in a price war with their Taiwanese and South Korean competitors.

The yen's rapid gains had a huge impact on the Japanese economy, where SMEs were hit the hardest, particularly those that relied on exports to America for much of their sales. The light manufacturing industry, with companies making such products as toys and music boxes, along with the textile industry, were unable to endure the pain. One after another, enterprises in these industries were forced to either change their business model or close up shop. This same pattern occurred with makers of Western-style tableware, which was one of the foremost industries in the city of Tsubame, also in Niigata Prefecture. And the story was repeated with SMEs in the neighboring city of Sanjo. Maruto Hasegawa would have surely suffered the same fate had it stood by and done nothing.

But as the company had done before the yen's appreciation, Maruto Hasegawa had been working to expand exports by serving a new market: Europe.

Maruto Hasegawa exhibited its products at tool expos in Germany. At a trade show, the Japanese company became acquainted with a German tool manufacturer that had a compelling suggestion: "Instead of selling your products at hardware stores, could you make us first-rate tools for professional use?" German edged tools have an established reputation for being the best in the world. Maruto Hasegawa took up the challenge of fashioning tools that would find acceptance among the well-respected German professionals. But after numerous attempts to upgrade its products, what it shipped was always rejected as being inadequate for use. Maruto Hasegawa saw more than just the difference between tools that sell well at hardware stores and those used by professionals at production sites; the company was also shown the great technological prowess of the Germans and the excellence of their products. It was a disheartening display, but never once did anybody at Maruto Hasegawa suggest giving up or think that the task before them was impossible. The great patience of the people of Niigata Prefecture, who must go about their lives buried under the snowfall for nearly half the year, was what paved the road to success.

From mass production to high quality

After more than three years, during which the company's new products were sent back for being "still inadequate" or "in need of further improvement," Maruto Hasegawa finally received a positive response. Masatoshi Kobayashi is a former Maruto Hasegawa employee who was then involved in the project as chief developer. It was a moving time for him. He said, "I can still vividly remember the deep emotions from that time. This is the joy one gets from making a living in manufacturing." Maruto Hasegawa's desperate efforts to satisfy the needs of a German company wanting a high-quality tool, coupled with the perseverance and patience to go through a trial-and-error process lasting more than three years, resulted in wire cutters that were not just the product of masterful skill in the narrow sense accepted in Japan, but were such a high grade that they earned global recognition as top-class implements. Maruto Hasegawa's decision to dramatically change course and become a maker of professional tools with high added value, rather than a mass producer, was what led to the company's current success.

According to President Naoya Hasegawa, "Perhaps the DNA of craftsmanship flows through the veins of the people of Niigata Prefecture and the folk from the Sanjo region." Indeed, as Naoya says, it is difficult to explain the three-year-long development project with the German company simply with patience and perseverance. The DNA of craftsmanship could very well be an important part of the story.

Maruto Hasegawa makes wire cutters that can even cut through piano wire. There are only a very few companies around the world that can fashion such sharp wire cutters, but these tools do more than just cut. Wire cutters are also used to cut components and raw materials at production sites that manufacture items like electronic devices and information appliances. A worker at one of these facilities will make thousands of cuts per day. Even taking just 0.5 seconds extra to execute a single cut can incur huge losses, impacting a factory's overall bottom line. What they need on the production floor is not just the ability to cut. The important thing is a tool that is long-lasting, plus a *kireaji* that dramatically reduces cutting time for workers. The wire cutters they use reduce cutting time to 0.5 seconds and can withstand between 50,000 and 100,000 cuts. That means they last for at least three weeks. There is a world of difference between a shoddy product that becomes useless in only a few days and the sharp-edged wire cutters made by Maruto Hasegawa. The company's exports to China and Southeast Asia are growing steadily due to the electronic device and information appliance industries' relocation of manufacturing operations to these places.

Masterful skill and selective use of raw materials

The company's proficient manufacture of wire cutters and other products begins with its selective use of the iron serving as the raw material. Kobe Steel, Ltd. produces a special raw iron for Maruto Hasegawa that includes miniscule amounts of rare metals. Kobe Steel has an established reputation as a maker of steel materials for special purposes. The steel produced with these techniques is one step toward creating a high-quality product. The next step is the forging process, by which the iron is imbued with strength by applying pressure with a massive 400-ton hammer. The forging process is a technique for increasing the strength of the metal by beating it under hundreds or thousands of tons of pressure. This removes hollowed spaces inside the metal and gives its crystallization a consistent orientation. The process has been used for centuries in Japan to craft swords. Even today, Japanese swords are highly acclaimed works of art that surpass ordinary blades.

The steel is heated at 1,000°C to shape the mold. Next comes 14 hours of annealing. The product could be made in less time, but a lengthier effort dramatically increases quality. It would be unthinkable for Maruto Hasegawa to deviate from this lengthy process. After this step, the material is shaved and otherwise machined to give the wire cutters their shape. Next is the quenching, which may be performed up to four times.

Following the quenching, high-precision machinery sharpens the edge in a special fabrication process. Veteran employees personally check each and every finished product. They use their eyes and experienced hands to test each wire cutter's cutting ability and to make sure there are no overall deformations, then make adjustments. They search for warping as small as one-thousandth of a millimeter and employ a simple tool to make the necessary adjustments. I am a layman in this field, so when they showed me their production site, I could not identify a deviation of one-thousandth of a millimeter at all. Most of the work is done by hand, so there are miniscule variations between each product. The only way to adjust for this is with masterful skills that have been cultivated through dedication.

Maruto Hasegawa entertains no thoughts of setting up production facilities overseas, as without the perseverance and indomitable spirit of Sanjo's artisans, the company never would have been able to produce high-quality products capable of competing with and besting those from other countries. President Naoya Hasegawa stated definitively, "Without the artisans of Sanjo, we couldn't make wire cutters with extraordinary *kireaji*." The word *kireaji* refers to more than just the ability to cut. It is something one feels, like a sixth sense. When Maruto Hasegawa manufactures a pair of wire cutters, it is something akin to the creation of a masterpiece. "Just like how even an [Italian or French] chef at a three-star restaurant cannot reproduce the subtle flavors of Japanese cuisine, our sharp wire cutters require the same quality." For that reason alone, the company values each and every worker, all of whom are permanent employees. There are no part-timers, student workers or temp. staff at Maruto Hasegawa. Although the company has made all-out efforts to streamline and otherwise reduce costs when the economy is slow, nobody has ever been laid off.

Many of the processes involved in manufacturing wire cutters—over 50—are performed by hand. Even so, Maruto Hasegawa is still not entirely content. The company has adopted the Toyota Production System, which has reduced the number of partly-finished goods prior to shipping from 960,000 a year to 180,000. If we assume each unit costs 200 yen, then that means a total cost-cutting effect of approximately 160 million yen. The job of replacing a die used in the forging process used to take half a day, but now that time has been shortened to only 6 minutes and 40 seconds. The company also succeeded in patiently convincing dealers to purchase nearly all exported items in Japanese yen, thus avoiding the risks of currency exchange fluctuations that even plague much larger companies.

Maruto Hasegawa is a 90-year-old enterprise, but it is looking ahead to 100 years in the future. It is for this reason that the company holds monthly study sessions for younger employees. Naoya, the president, also attends but does not speak at the sessions. Instead, he allows his workers to engage in open discussion. The company has also applied its proficiency with wire cutters to enter the business of wire cutter-shaped nail clippers, or "nail nippers." Maruto Hasegawa aims to use its level of *kireaji* to capture demand for nail clippers that it anticipates from beauticians. It also projects substantial need for wire cutter-shaped nail clippers with the kind of sharpness that it has worked to refine over many years in its wire-cutter business. This bold attitude of an unwavering and tireless pursuit of betterment and exploring new opportunities is also part of Maruto Hasegawa's DNA.

An SME from Ube with a 70% global market share

Kanikama, literally "crab sticks" or more often called "imitation crab meat" in English, provide consumers with an affordable way to enjoy the taste of otherwise pricey crab. They are sold in supermarkets as far away from Japan as Europe. Crab sticks are a familiar food to the Japanese, but did you know that in France, consumption of imitation crab meat outpaces that in Japan? Furthermore, the world's largest imitation crab meat company is in Eastern Europe, in the country of Lithuania. America's consumption of the food is also greater than Japan's. A seafood sandwich in France is sure to contain this food product. Nearly half of Italian seafood pasta also uses it. Many readers of this book may find it hard to believe, but these facts are all true.

The company that dominates the market for imitation crab meat machines, with a share of around 70%, and which has helped spread the technology worldwide, has its headquarters located in the city of Ube, Yamaguchi Prefecture. It has a capitalization of 100 million yen and employs 150 people. The name of this SME is Yanagiya Machinery Co., Ltd.

In Japan we often use the term *kanikama* and that is in reference to crab sticks, but elsewhere in the world this imitation crab meat, which comes in many shapes and sizes, is commonly called "surimi." Yoshio Yanagiya, the company's president, speculates that the term "surimi" came about during an informational session to market fish paste products like *kanikama*. People from non-Japanese companies were also in attendance and "perhaps they just started using a word they heard the Japanese using: *surimi*." In Japanese, the word *surimi* has a broader meaning that is literally "ground meat." Along with words like "sushi" and "tempura," "surimi," as a synonym for *kanikama*, is one of the few Japanese terms to have gained global currency.

Products made with Yanagiya machinery and sold in overseas markets

CHAPTER 1

In 1989, global *kanikama* production volume was no more than 150,000 tons, of which around 50,000 tons was made in Japan. However, production gradually and steadily grew to 300,000 tons in 1996 and then to 400,000 tons in 2004. Today that number has reached 500,000 tons. And yet despite global production volume increasing by nearly four times in the span of about 25 years, Japanese production has remained fairly steady at 50,000 tons; it hasn't increased at all. Why is that?

The reason is that massive gains in production have occurred in Europe, primarily in the eastern part of the continent.

Until 1989, Europe accounted for only about 10% of global production. That share began to shoot up in or around 1992, reaching roughly half of global output in 2000 and roughly two-thirds now. Lithuania makes 80,000 tons of *kanikama* a year, more than the 55,000 tons produced in Japan. France makes 50,000 tons a year, roughly on par with Japan. Several countries have production volume in excess of 10,000 tons: 41,000 tons in Russia, 15,000 tons in Spain and 13,000 tons in Belarus. Meanwhile, America has an output of 77,000 tons, 40% more than Japan's production capacity. The story elsewhere is 45,000 tons in Thailand and 42,000 tons in China. Other *kanikama*-producing countries with output of less than 10,000 tons range from those in Eastern Europe and other countries on the continent such as Italy, Ukraine and Poland, to nations in Central and South America like Brazil and Argentina. Most of the *kanikama* machines in these countries are supplied by Yanagiya. Although nothing more than an SME from Ube, Yanagiya is a global brand.

A long road to dispel a bad reputation

Yanagiya's current president, Yoshio Yanagiya, is responsible for turning a small factory making *kamaboko* (fish cake) machines into a global enterprise. The company's roots trace back to the *kamaboko* shop his grandfather, Motosuke Yanagiya, opened in Ube in 1916. At the time, *kamaboko* was made by hand and the work of grinding the fish meat was a laborious task requiring tremendous energy. After trying many ways to make this work even a little bit easier, Motosuke succeeded in creating an electric machine for which he then filed a utility model patent application. After patenting an upgraded version of this grinding kneader, he established a company to build the machine: Yanagiya Iron Works. Motosuke is recognized for his contributions to the *kamaboko* industry and his efforts to develop the broader seafood processing industry. In 1955 he was presented with the Medal with Yellow Ribbon, a Medal of Honor awarded by the government of Japan, for his ideas for and improvements to seafood processing machinery and his contributions to their development. When he passed away two years later, in 1957, Yoshio's father Yukio took the company's reins.

Yukio became the chairman 18 years later and transferred the post of president to his eldest son, Yoshio. Although Yoshio was still only 25 years old at the time, Yanagiya's share of the local market in Yamaguchi Prefecture was only around 20%. Yoshio targeted *kamaboko* companies and other marine products enterprises that were current or promising future customers, beginning within the prefecture. He spent five years promoting the company's sales at the highest level. But what he heard during this time was negative feedback: "Your price is too high"; "Maintenance is bad"; "The machine performs poorly."

An ordinary business manager might have thrown in the towel or lost all motivation, but Yoshio saw this as an opportunity. He adopted some positive thinking: "Our market share is low, so there's plenty of room for us to grow. If our machines are bad, then they'll be happy to buy if we can make good ones. If there's a problem with maintenance, then we should improve our service."

It does not bear repeating, but *kanikama* is not real crab, but rather a product with crab flavor made from the ground meat of cod and other fish. The first generation of *kanikama* were shaped like sticks; the second generation were high-quality products that were diagonally cut and processed from sheets of intermediate ingredients; the third generation was the natural type; and today's fourth generation comes in the *kaori bako* ("aromatic box") style. It is a food that has evolved over time. In fact, its appearance and flavor so closely resemble genuine crab that packages are now printed with a label declaring, "This is not crab."

The first-generation *kanikama* gained popularity around the time that Yoshio became president and began traveling around Japan. He directed all efforts toward developing a *kanikama* machine that his intuition told him would "revolutionize the *kamaboko* industry." Then, in 1979, the company developed the Imitation Crab Meat Plant that would go on to be a global hit. In 1982 the company developed the Ball Cutter that processes *kamaboko* ingredients at high speed inside a vacuum. Yanagiya's business performance recovered by exporting a single set containing ingredient processing equipment and the Imitation Crab Meat Plant. This event marked the beginning of Yanagiya as a global enterprise.

The machinery whips up the fish meat to grind it, stretches it into sheets about 1 mm thick, then leaves a "skin" about 0.1 mm thick. This keeps the product from falling apart. When the sheets are then turned into a twisted fiber (called *koyori* in

Japanese), this gives the *kanikama* enhanced flavor. Tomato is used to add red coloring in a technique that gave birth to "real *kanikama*" that is indistinguishable from genuine crab.

These days in the United States, where the annual *kanikama* production of approximately 80,000 tons exceeds that in Japan, the product is marketed as Crab Flavored Seafood. In 2013, Yanagiya concluded a contract to sell *kanikama* production lines to America's largest seafood company. American product inspections are extremely strict. If bacteria or other foreign matter is mixed in with a food product, it can hurt a company's image so badly that it could go out of business. So the most important thing for food product machinery is cleaning. When Yanagiya delivers a product, engineers from the seafood company will come and conduct a thorough inspection.

The engineers say that the reason why they chose to order Yanagiya's machines is that Yanagiya has the best global name recognition, the company is known for the technological prowess it has cultivated over its long history and the after-sales services is also thorough. They also spoke highly of the Techno (the latest *kanikama*) Yanagiya's machines produce, calling it very close to the real thing. The engineers emphasize their gratitude for how Yanagiya has done an incredible job in making excellent machinery. Yanagiya has climbed to the top of the industry by developing its *kanikama* technology. It would not go too far to say that the history tracing the company's development of its machines is synonymous with the history of *kanikama*'s evolution. The following example should demonstrate why.

Better-tasting than the handmade product

Based on the company's extensive experience, Yanagiya has set the following four points as its business policy:

1. Do what nobody else does.
2. Be a company others cannot do without.
3. Know everything about our work.
4. Offer solutions that are one step ahead of the competition.

As *kanikama* began selling more in Japan, fish was gaining attention elsewhere in the world as a healthy food. Japanese *kamaboko* makers took notice of this trend and exported their products to Western countries and elsewhere across the globe, thus enabling the rapid popularization of *kanikama*. The lack of bones helped it find acceptance among Westerners who have relatively fewer opportunities to dine on fish. Furthermore, the vivid red design also helped *kanikama* become a hit. Yanagiya first exported its Imitation Crab Meat Plant in 1982, to South Korea. Because this machinery had roughly the same production capacity as models used in Japan, sealing the deal was a smooth process. However, when discussing deals with customers in the Eastern European country of Lithuania, not only did Yanagiya's counterparts want to vastly surpass Japan's production volume, but Yanagiya also faced numerous obstacles the company had never before experienced.

The first problem was the language barrier. Furthermore, at that time most Japanese companies had never done business in Lithuania before and Yanagiya had little information about the country's economy, industry or infrastructure. After hearing that the hotels around the factory construction site were not satisfactory, President Yoshio Yanagiya was for a time hesitant to proceed with discussions. Yanagiya does not just sell machines; the company installs the machinery at the factory and verifies that it is operating properly before handing it over to the customer. There was plenty to be concerned about in this case. Would the machinery move properly in the completely different conditions and climate of Lithuania? When fine-tuning the machines, would Yanagiya's people be able to communicate well with the Lithuanian technicians? But Yanagiya began exporting to Lithuania because it is a company that will "Do what nobody else does." "There were many issues," according to President Yoshio Yanagiya, but the fruits of Yanagiya's toils created what is today the largest *kanikama* factory in the world.

In addition to its Imitation Crab Meat Plant, Yanagiya makes many kinds of food machinery for producing *kamaboko*, tofu, soy bean milk and dried seaweed. Drying seaweeds to make *nori* requires such extremely subtle adjustments that venerable *nori* companies still use traditional methods out of the belief that "You can't create authentic *nori* flavors without making it by hand." Enterprises that have been in business since the Edo Period insisted on producing their *nori* by hand, but Yanagiya was able to sell its seaweed drying machines to these companies when their veteran employees gave their stamp of approval by asserting that even handmade *nori* could not taste better. The resulting reputation Yanagiya's machinery earned for processing delicious *nori* led a major convenience store chain to use the company's seaweed drying machinery for all the *nori* wrapping the rice balls on its shelves.

"We're not trying to be Toyota."

The Great East Japan Earthquake inflicted the heaviest damage along the coast of the Sanriku region, primarily in Miyagi Prefecture and Iwate Prefecture. The region is known for its concentration of companies that process ground fish meat into *kanikama*, as well as *kamaboko* and other deep-fried foods. Over 120 firms here are Yanagiya customers. After the earthquake struck, President Yoshio Yanagiya immediately directed the staff at his Sendai sales office to "visit places like Shiogama and report to me on how our customers are doing." Although the tsunami had pushed seawater up to the office's entrance, the premises received no direct damage from the monstrous wave. However, nearby roads were cluttered with garbage, scrap wood and other debris that rendered automobiles useless. Kazuto Arita, the office manager, started using a bicycle to make his rounds of the customers. Apparently, many of the presidents and top executives at these client businesses were stunned that Arita had rushed out to visit them when many companies still had not even prepared for the cleanup. In the end, all these companies' factories were deemed incapable of starting up production again, either because the tsunami had completely or significantly destroyed the factories, or because seawater and mud had gotten stuck in the production machinery.

When Yoshio heard about this, he formed a special machinery repair team which he immediately dispatched to the disaster zone. The repair technicians were under strict orders: "When you take a maintenance job, do not speak a word about money." Yoshio sent out his best technicians because "our company's machines are like our children. When their children are in trouble, parents of course provide help. Besides, these companies are in a life-and-death situation." But when the technicians arrived, they found unusable machinery clogged with seawater and mud, or entire factories destroyed, along with their electrical systems. No matter how fast they conducted the repairs, it was thought that most of the machines would need at least half a year to come back online. To make things worse, they were unable to arrange for the cranes needed to lift up heavy machinery weighing upward of 100 kg.

Machines that were rusted from seawater or damaged by mud had to be repaired by hand one at a time. The repairs were a job that meant getting covered in mud. The repair team had a motto: "Work as fast as possible." As a result of the team's efforts, at some companies the team was able to complete installations in a month and then restart production half a month thereafter. One of Yanagiya's customers expressed a sentiment shared by many others: "If our operations are delayed, then warehouses and retailers will get replacements from other companies. That would have a huge impact on our business, so I'm so happy I could cry." Yanagiya's machines are renowned for their simple operation. For example, they are incredibly easy to clean and that is of the greatest importance when it comes to food machinery. Why? "Sometimes part-timers or student workers operate food machinery. If they aren't easy to operate, then that could cause breakdowns or other problems."

"We don't aspire to be a gigantic global company like Toyota." Although the market is small, Yanagiya's goal is to be a firm with products its customers cannot do without. And although the company has an overwhelmingly dominant share of the global market, it is always exploring new opportunities "because five or ten years from now, there could be a new product that replaces *kanikama*." Yanagiya is nearing its 100th year in business, but the goal is to remain a successful enterprise, as it is today, a century from now.

400 years of history and tradition is not refuge enough

AWA SPINDLE CO., LTD. is a manufacturer of spindles, which are crucial components in textile machinery for making clothing. The company's head office is located in the city of Yoshinogawa, nearly an hour by car from Tokushima Awaodori Airport in Tokushima Prefecture. This local SME has 130 employees, 48 million yen in capital and annual sales of 2.3 billion yen. Until a few years ago, the Awa brand was all over the global textile market, but in terms of volume the brand has lost its global top share due to the ability of countries like China and South Korea to produce cheap products in large quantities.

Textiles encompass many different kinds of products. They can be categorized into natural fibers like cotton, wool, hemp and silk, synthetic fibers such as polyester, nylon and acryl and chemical fibers including staple fiber and artificial silk (both of which are otherwise known as rayon). All of these fibers have one thing in common: after the raw material is twisted into a thread or otherwise processed, it is used as fabric or yarn for producing the clothing that is the end product. Synthetic fibers are the mainstream raw materials today. If we explore their use in textile manufacturing more closely, we see the role that spindles play: they quickly wind thread that has been produced by passing raw polyester or nylon through the thin tube of a nozzle. From the time of the first spinning wheel to the textiles produced in the Edo Period, the spindles in use were nothing more than simple metal implements, but with the development of the textile industry, they have come to be vital components that make its modern incarnation feasible.

Although the textile industry is considered to be in decline, it would be no exaggeration to say that it built the foundations for the development of the modern Japanese economy. At first Japan relied on textile machinery imported from overseas, but the country began making its own machinery, starting with the automatic looms for fibers and fabrics produced by Toyota and Suzuki. Awa Spindle achieved growth as a maker of the crucial nozzles and spindles used as parts by Japan's textile and textile machinery industries.

A growing business in a booming industry

Awa Spindle once had a large quantity of precious documents in its possession, including written texts from centuries ago, but a company president from several generations back had most of them burned, as they were deemed unnecessary. Therefore we only have oral information passed down generation to generation by the company's owners, but according to CEO Masahiko Kimura (it is the company rule not to call him "President," unlike many companies in Japan), "The *tsumu*, or molds for the critical spindles and nozzles used in textile machinery, were important parts from time immemorial—back when looms were incredibly simple contraptions made of wood—so they were probably simple rods made from metal." Then, around the year 1800, during the Edo Period, the fourth-generation head of the company, Nabe-emon, crossed the sea from Shikoku to the neighboring island of Kyushu and traveled to Nagasaki. There he learned from a Dutch engineer about carburizing, which was an advanced technique at the time, so he could bring this knowledge back to his business and make more durable spindles with harder metal.

This development set the enterprise on the path to mass production. The seventh-generation owner, Shohei, organized the business to handle a greater volume of sales and embarked upon mass production. In 1868, the first year of the Meiji Period, Shohei established a business called Kimura Shohei Shoten that began producing spindles. This shop was the beginning of the modern-day Awa Spindle. It began by producing the same spindles Shohei's family had been making for over 200 years, since the early days of the Edo Period, but then reoriented its business for the full-scale manufacture of spindles at the dawn of the Meiji Period, as Japan was transforming into a modern state.

Unlike today's spindles, those produced at that time were simple devices. In 1919 the company changed its name to Awa Tsumu Seisakusho. As the Japanese word for "spindle" is *tsumu*, we can speculate from this new name that the company still primarily produced spindles. Meanwhile, due to growing demand stemming from a textile industry that was thriving across Japan, the company began manufacturing spindles for imported twisted yarn machines made in Italy. It expanded its factory in 1927 and spread its sales network nationwide.

In the turbulent years following the end of World War II, the company expanded beyond spindles into the manufacture of farm implements and other products. In 1954, after the situation in Japan had become more orderly and the country's economy had begun to grow, the enterprise adopted the name it carries today: Awa Spindle. This was a major step toward becoming a business specializing in spindles. In 1967, as Japan's post-war economic boom was running full steam ahead, Awa Spindle built a new production facility at the New Sezume Factory, which had a total floor space of 3,250 square meters. This was followed the next year by the construction of the New Main Factory, with a floor space of 1,700 square meters. These new manufacturing centers provided a jolt for the company's production. Awa Spindle felt compelled to grow because "companies like Toray and Teijin had built synthetic fiber factories nearby." Toray was the first Japanese company to manufacture synthetic nylon. Soon after nylon manufacturing commenced, the nylon business expanded beyond clothing to provide materials used by a range of industries, where new applications for nylon were being developed at a rapid clip.

Toray's booming business pushed many companies like Teijin, Asahi Kasei and Mitsubishi Rayon that produced chemical fibers, including artificial silk and staple fiber, to begin making such synthetic fibers as nylon, polyester and acryl. Synthetic fibers later on replaced natural fibers and established a central presence in the textile industry. Many of the main factories were concentrated in regions like Shikoku (where Awa Spindle is based) and Kinki. Meanwhile, production volume grew rapidly from the 1960s to the 1970s.

A swarm of counterfeit makers

Nozzles and spindles like those made by Awa Spindles are essential to the production of these synthetic fibers. Textiles made with synthetic fibers are created by squeezing raw plastic into yarn. This yarn is twisted and false-twisted, then used in the weaving, dyeing and selling processes to produce the final product. During manufacture, nozzles do more than just applying a uniform coat of oil to half-finished products of squeezed uncut threads: the nozzles also process the threads to make the yarn easy to remove during winding. Spindles, meanwhile, come in two types. One winds while twisting thread. The other winds the yarn onto a bobbin as it rotates. Naturally, makers of synthetic fibers ask a lot from their nozzles and spindles so as to not only boost production volume, but also to improve quality. To give synthetic fiber manufacturers what they want, Awa Spindle worked to improve precision and increase production volume.

Today the company's false-twisting spindles rotate at a speed of 1 million revolutions per minute. In the synthetic fiber industry, machinery operates 24 hours a day. But even under such extreme conditions, these false-twisting spindles last four to five years. If operated at a slower speed of around 30,000 revolutions per minute, they can be used for 15 to 20 years.

Meanwhile, from fashioning the raw materials into thin threads to the manufacture of the final yarn, synthetic fibers are produced at a rate of 6,000 meters per minute. That is equal to 360 km/h, an incredible speed that is faster than a bullet train. Awa Spindle is the only company anywhere in the world capable of making nozzles and spindles that can keep up with this rapid pace of synthetic fiber manufacture. The enterprise has become a top global company due to the many highly-skilled and knowledgeable employees who are involved in making these nozzles and spindles that are indispensable to textile production: from the design phase to the manufacturing process.

There are five people in the company's long history who have made particularly notable contributions to its growth. Two of them accomplished their deeds during the Edo Period: Nabe-emon, the fourth-generation proprietor, and Shohei, the seventh in his line. Another is Tamejuro, the eighth-generation owner who achieved a huge leap forward in production volume by using electricity to automate manufacturing operations and who laid the foundations for the enterprise as we know it today. Next is Seiji, who vastly expanded the business by developing spindles compatible with synthetic fibers. He also earned Awa Spindle the Corporate Exporter Contribution Award from the Ministry of International Trade and Industry (the predecessor to today's Ministry of Economy, Trade and Industry) for the company's efforts to promote imports. The fifth and final of these distinguished figures is Satoru, the eleventh head of Awa Spindle, who worked hard to increase imports to places where the textile industry had recently developed, such as South Korea and Taiwan, and established Awa as a global brand in the textile business.

According to an industry insider, there are "up to 13 companies in China alone" that sell counterfeit Awa products. There is also a considerable number of counterfeit good makers in countries with developed textile industries, like India and China, that brazenly pretend to sell Awa brand products.

Within the industry there is no end of jokes of the black humor variety about Awa Spindle. For example, when Awa Spindle sales reps visit an overseas textile maker, they may be greeted with the refrain, "Hey, didn't your company just come to try and sell me something the other day?"

Another way to take this counterfeiting would be to see it as evidence of the power and respect the Awa Spindle brand still commands globally. At the same time, as he focused on foreign markets, Satoru succeeded in beefing up the company's domestic sales network by opening the Hokuriku Service Station in Fukui Prefecture, which is a major center of the textile industry in the Hokuriku region of Japan.

A resignation accompanied by a promise to reform

However, the manufacture of nozzles and spindles has become a thriving business in developing countries and in China. Although Awa Spindle's technology is the best in the world right now, in terms of sales volume the company is not the global leader. Nothing compares with the quality of Awa Spindle's products, but makers in places like China and in developing countries have used low prices to put up fierce competition. The situation in the industry is like a state of civil war between multiple parties, with no company able to gain dominance. But Awa Spindle has come up with a plan to regain the top spot under these circumstances. There are two types of nozzles: air jet nozzles and water jet nozzles. Air jet nozzles require more sophisticated engineering and there are specialized manufacturers in Europe with the advanced technology and large product lineups. Awa Spindle's goal is to surpass these companies in a few years, or to at least stand shoulder-to-shoulder with them.

Meanwhile, the company has been working since 2009 to remake its business in a "second founding" of the company. As part of this initiative, the company is developing new products based on the core technologies it has created through the manufacture of spindles. One example is the components for machine analyzers that employ lasers and are made with the rotor production technology Awa Spindle uses to maintain unwavering balance, even when rotating at 1 million revolutions per minute. Another is the application of microfabrication techniques to create components used in the ultra-precise fabrication of sapphires and other materials. Awa Spindle uses a centralized center for managing business information—from product acceptance to orders, design, development and delivery—and this has begun to show results by cutting production costs and reducing the occurrence of defects. The company has trained its personnel so well that many of the technicians have passed proficiency tests to earn certifications, with four of them recognized as Class 1 technicians and 46 as Class 2 technicians.

The global financial crisis that began with the collapse of Lehman Brothers was a large part of the impetus behind the decision to remake the company. Awa Spindle's goal is to go from being an SME to a medium-sized enterprise by 2018, 150 years after the company's initial founding. To that end, in 2010 the company formulated the Fifth Mid-Term Business Plan. Awa Spindle's objective is to pivot toward selling consulting services, while utilizing its ingenuity and wisdom and thoroughly eliminating all waste to earn a profit even when prices drop by 50%. CEO Masahiko Kimura has declared that he will step down in 2018. He is managing the company as if he is fighting with his back to the wall: "If my term in this post is set, then I can implement reforms and improvements with unflagging resolve."

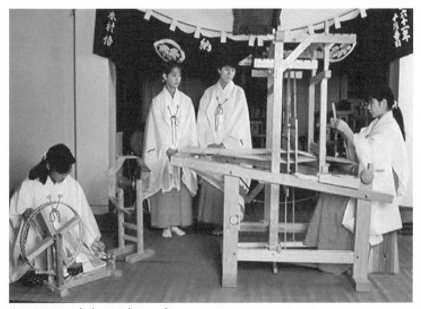

A ceremony in which aratae hemp jackets are woven

Traditions maintained and passed down

According to a pamphlet written by Satoru Kimura, the current chairman, it is thought that the techniques behind the company's textile production were passed down by the Kamiyo Inbe people who lived in the Yoshinogawa area well over a millennium ago. This part of Shikoku where Awa Spindle is presently located was once known by the name Oe. According to *Oe no densetsu* [The Legend of Oe], long ago, spinning wheel builders were placed here so the god of the Inbe could spin hemp. Thus, among the Inbe, the house of Tani (now the Kimura family) prospered by manufacturing spinning wheels. Furthermore, according to a passage from the *Amenohi washinomiya engi*, the written history of Inbe Shrine, "This house produced spinning wheels. Long ago, so that the great deity Inbe could spin hemp, spinning wheel builders were placed in this village and made to construct these tools."

Later, whenever a new emperor ascended the Chrysanthemum Throne, the descendants of the Inbe would provide a gift of hemp fabrics. During the *Daijosai*, the first ceremonial offering of rice to the current Emperor of Japan when he assumed his position in November 1990, Awa Spindle presented him with four *aratae* jackets of hemp, which were used at his coronation. As was done long ago, girls dressed as shrine maidens wove fabrics with wooden spinning wheels and looms according to the ancient method. Thus, we can conjecture that what we call a "legend" actually contains much historical fact. Awa Spindle CEO Masahiko Kimura declares that "my role is to maintain and pass down these traditions." Compared to other countries, Japan has many very old enterprises that are still in business. According to credit research firm Tokyo Shoko Research, Japan has 158 companies that have been in existence for at least 500 years. The oldest is said to be Kongo Gumi, in Osaka, which was involved in the construction of Horyu-ji, a temple that is one of the oldest wooden buildings in the world. However, Awa Spindle has not only tradition but also great potential to write yet more history. Furthermore, the company possesses some of the most advanced spindle technology in the world and has embarked on a push to regain the top share of the global market. Although it is a venerable business that has tremendously old traditions, the desire to take on new challenges remains strong and healthy.

Discovering new opportunities for die & mold powerhouse Japan

Japan was once a powerhouse in the business of dies and molds used in manufacturing, with a global market share of over 40%. However, due to automakers, home appliance manufacturers and others relocating their production operations overseas and because of competition by inferior, low-cost dies produced by companies from other countries, the number of die and mold businesses operating in Japan has dropped by 40% from its heyday. According to statistics provided by the Japan Die & Mold Industry Association, the number of business establishments and the value of their production output have both steadily fallen. Orders for dies and molds experienced a particularly devastating drop during the global financial crisis. When it struck in 2009, the value of these orders suddenly dropped to 1.159 trillion yen, or 31.7% below the previous year. There was somewhat of a recovery thereafter, but the value of orders was still stagnant by 2012, as they were worth 1.2505 trillion yen. This was only around 60% of the business this industry was doing at its peak in 1991, when it handled business worth 1.9575 trillion yen.

According to people in the die and mold industry, the biggest cause for its decline has been intense competition with overseas manufacturers in China and developing countries who have cheap labor, along with loud demands for discounts by parent companies. In addition, because it is typical industry practice to set the price of dies and molds according to their weight, it is not uncommon for technological advances that lower weight to result in price reductions. This explains the smoldering resentment in the die and mold industry for the general lack of respect for their technology. I heard one industry insider lament, "I suppose even more companies will pull out of the business in the future."

But although the business environment is getting worse, UMIX CO., LTD., a maker of dies located in Hirakata, Osaka Prefecture, produces high-performance dies that other companies cannot replicate and is doing better business thanks to direct orders from major overseas automakers.

80% of sales come from overseas

While many die manufacturers are desperately struggling to stay alive, Umix was quick to start dealing directly with customers outside Japan. The company's net sales are 2.59 billion yen, of which around 80% comes from overseas. At one time that proportion was closer to 90%, but the company corrected that as it perceived an over-reliance on foreign markets. Even so, at 80%, overseas sales still account for quite a large share. As Umix President Koji Temma explains, "Japanese manufacturers prioritize price over technology. Since they don't give us much recognition for our advanced engineering, we weighted more of our sales efforts toward foreign customers." As his words indicate, there are some who think very highly of his company's dies.

In May 2014, Daimler, the maker of Mercedes-Benz automobiles, began producing the W205, its new C-Class automobile, in South Africa. This C-Class was the first model for Daimler to produce on four continents (with manufacturing operations in Germany, America, South Africa and China) and it was the first such case in South Africa. Umix dies are used in the manufacture of the vehicle's parts. Daimler sent Umix a gracious letter of thanks for making this project successful. That same letter also asked for Umix's continued cooperation in the future.

Umix's main customers in the United States are the so-called "big three" American automakers: Chrysler, Ford and General Motors. In Europe they are Daimler, BMW, Audi, Opel, Volvo and Volkswagen. Meanwhile, in Asia, Umix's primary customers include Hyundai Motor, Daimler (China), BMW (China) and General Motors (Thailand). Umix also does business in Japan with clients such as Toyota and Daihatsu, but as mentioned earlier, in terms of monetary value the lion's share of business is with overseas makers.

Umix's dealings outside Japan are carried out directly, without going through a trading firm. This is why, despite being an SME with 110 employees, the company has set up local subsidiaries for technical service support and sales in America and Germany, with 12 people stationed in the U.S. and 3 in Germany. Umix also manufactures some products locally in the United States.

Since many SMEs do not have information or sales networks, they have no choice but to rely on the big trading firms for their dealings outside Japan. Certainly, the salespeople at these trading firms put a lot of effort into moving large products worth hundreds of millions or billions of yen, but how much do they devote to selling relatively less expensive products like dies that are designed for incredibly specialized uses? This is an unknown. Therefore, Umix has followed its philosophy of "selling technological skill and service" by setting up local subsidiaries in Europe, the birthplace of the automobile industry, and in America, one of the world's leading car-producing countries. These moves have supported the enterprise's growth. In Japan, parent companies try to draw manufacturing subcontractors who make exceptional parts into their fold by forming organizations such as *kyoryokukai* (meaning "cooperative group"). In Western countries, though, engineers involved in automobile manufacturing often take jobs at rival firms and those engineers who used Umix's fine dies continue to do so when they go to another employer.

Another thing about Western countries is that engineers get together and interact with each other without worrying about the names of the companies they work for. It is perfectly natural to hear them share information like, "Umix dies vastly improved sales of our cars and allowed us to produce wonderful vehicles." One good thing about Western countries is that they do not fixate on a company's name recognition or size. In Japan, it is not rare for a big company to turn away a no-name startup or SME at the reception desk when its sales reps come to sell an excellent product that their company has developed. However, in Western countries it is common business practice to deal with unknown companies, so long as they can meet the strict conditions of the order, such as product quality and delivery deadlines.

In fact, there are numerous cases of Japanese SMEs growing into global enterprises in a niche area after earning great respect from foreign companies before anyone else because even though they were making great products, nobody in Japan would do business with them. Umix follows Western business practices by also taking care of its "engineers in the field," not just the salespeople who deal with customers. The way Umix has developed its business is vastly different from other Japanese die manufacturers, but Umix has boosted its reputation overseas while also increasing sales. That is something to be commended.

How to deal with pressure to lower prices

Umix was not always a company that possessed advanced technology that amazed overseas manufacturers. Toshihiro Uemura, who had worked at Matsushita Electric Industrial (known today as Panasonic), created the company in 1945 during the chaotic aftermath of World War II. He started out making dies for light electrical appliances. After building on the company's technical prowess, he began manufacturing automobile dies in 1967. Thanks to an expansive personal network and salesmanship, Uemura won contracts from companies like Mazda and Mitsubishi Motors. Although his business mostly made interior parts, it had already established its engineering capabilities, as exemplified by the fact that Uemura served for 10 years as the chairman of Daihatsu's cooperative group for jigs and dies.

An often-cited reason why the enterprise earned such a great reputation as a subcontractor is due to a certain individual with great technical skill who suddenly joined the company and developed high-quality dies. Another factor behind the success would probably be that Uemura directed the profits he earned from light electrical appliance dies to developing auto-related technology.

In 1967 the company changed its name to Uemura Kinzoku Kogyo. It was around this time that it made a major pivot, shifting its focus from light electrical appliance dies to automobiles. There was another name change in 1990 to Umix, still in use now, to enhance the company's image after it began doing serious business in Western countries. Up until the 1960s, many Japanese citizens aspired to own a (black and white) TV, an electrically-powered refrigerator and a washing machine. By the 1970s most of them had these appliances and so they then began to desire the so-called "three Cs": a car, a cooler (in reference to an air-conditioning unit) and a color TV. However, national income increased during the postwar boom, while Japanese automakers released numerous models that were affordable for the typical consumer. As the popularization of the automobile spread quickly in Japan, the period defined by personal automobile ownership arrived in the late 1970s. Umix was right to shift from household appliance components to auto parts, as the auto business grew to play a leading role in Japanese industry.

Where Umix did miscalculate was the assumption that extremely low prices for parts made by the auto industry's subcontractors meant Umix would be constantly pressed to lower its prices. In response to the rapid appreciation of the yen from the 1980s and 1990s, Japanese industry called for an all-out effort to reduce costs. Automakers were particularly zealous in their cost-cutting pursuits. Japan's automobile subcontractors tried desperately to cope, but more than a few were forced to step away from the business and close up shop. This situation led Umix to the decision to focus its business overseas and cater to "companies that admire our engineering and will buy dies at fair prices." The company now has dealings with major automakers from around the world, receives high praise for "making excellent products" and is growing its business. Umix's strategy of steadfastly sticking to its guns and "getting companies to buy our technology at fair prices" has been a resounding success and it was made possible due to the company's technological prowess.

Still better than a 3D printer

The RotaryCam is one piece of die technology the company is especially proud of. Conventional die making to produce stamped parts involves cutting a single sheet of steel and using dies at several different stages. The RotaryCam, however, employs a method that makes the stamped part easy to extract by rotating the "formed parts with negative angles," which are embedded in places that are unreachable by presses that simply move up and down. This cuts what is normally a six-step process down to four steps. Although this achievement may seem to be of minor significance, it can result in massive cost reductions. Japanese automakers, however, passed on adopting the technique because it had "no track record," so the first to put it into practice was a Taiwanese maker. Now, though, it is in use by many automakers around the world because it contributes directly to lower costs.

There is a growing opinion that 3D printers will fundamentally change manufacturing because when used in combination with a computer, one can send and receive complex three-dimensional drawings. This was not possible before. Umix began using 3D technology as long as 16 years ago, when it was not even topical, because of the engineer who first noticed it and whose intuition said "this could massively transform the future of manufacturing." When Umix talks with overseas manufacturers, it mostly does so based on three-dimensional designs produced with 3D printer technology. But a policy of making dies based solely on these 3D designs would be unthinkable.

3D printer technology has made rapid advances. Recently, there was a stir in Japan over a newspaper story about a man who had been arrested for making a pistol with a 3D printer, but making one product at a time based on a 3D printer design takes time and incurs high costs. That is because 3D printers still have a long way to go before they can catch up with Umix's die technology that can mass-produce high-quality products one at a time and at low cost.

Umix excels at high-precision dies. One product category they are used for is auto parts, like doors and the front fenders, which are defining elements of a car's style. In order to fabricate these parts with great precision, the die maker must meet many times with automaker engineers to work out all the details, no matter how minor. Sometimes this happens when a Umix employee goes to visit the manufacturer, or they meet next to a large press at a Umix factory.

Automakers are shifting to steel and high-tensile steel plates to make lighter cars with better gas mileage and less environmental impact. Japan's steelmakers are proud of the high-tensile steel plates they produce because they represent some of the best technology in the world, as they are very strong yet thin and lightweight.

Another one of Umix's leading products is a piece of manufacturing equipment called the JCM SlideCam. This patented machinery is used in the fabrication of high-tensile steel plates. In addition to producing strong plates and being very safe, the JCM SlideCam is designed to run silently so as to reduce noise in a stamping plant. Thus it has earned high marks for helping to cut noise pollution.

Another notable thing about Umix is how incredibly small its administrative staff is. While the company has 4 executives, 78 production personnel, 25 engineering and design team members, 4 developers and 10 sales and purchasing staff members, the administrative department that handles accounting, human resources and other general affairs has only 3 workers. President Temma used to work in the accounting department. Since "back in my time one person was enough," he has kept the administrative team from growing in size and has meanwhile assigned nearly one-fourth of the workforce to engineering and design work that directly contributes to improving product performance. This is due to Umix's focus on technology and development. It is clearly an enterprise with a thorough passion for technology. As the majority of sales come from overseas, Umix has always provided company information and product pamphlets in both Japanese and English. Its English-language website leads directly to inquiries from outside Japan. As Umix plans to continue increasing profits by expanding its business abroad, the company is now getting more applications from graduates of top universities in the field of linguistics because they "want to use their language skills."

Energy consumption savings + shorter fabrication times

While the Japanese language uses one word, *kanagata*, English differentiates between the two broad categories of *kanagata* with separate terms: metal dies for making metal products and plastic molds for making plastic products. While Umix is a manufacturer of metal dies, KTX Corporation is a maker of plastic molds for automobile interiors. Headquartered in the city of Konan, Aichi Prefecture, it has 158 employees and annual sales of 4.3 billion yen. Although KTX is thought of as a local SME, the perforating molds the company makes with its electroforming technology (porous electroforming, to be specific) provide a big boost to both energy savings and efficiency, while also producing molded products of extremely high quality. Thus, KTX's molds have been used by Japanese automakers as well as numerous leading car manufacturers across the globe.

Japan's Ministry of Economy, Trade and Industry has listed this company among the "top 300 manufacturing SMEs building a brighter future for Japan" and the "top 100 global niche companies," the reason in both cases being KTX's proprietary porous electroforming technology for automobile interiors. Clearly, this technology has earned a good reputation. Current President Yasuyoshi Noda built up the company in one generation.

KTX independently developed its plastic forming molds with Porous

Electroforming®, a technology for opening holes in molds. Although it is patent-protected, many companies have employed technology that gets around the patent to try and make the same kind of product. But KTX says that what is more important is that "we not only have patent protection, but also the know-how we have built up over many years." KTX keeps details of the engineering and the knowledge under tight control as the most important of company secrets.

What we do know for sure, though, is that KTX opens holes only microns wide in its molds. Plastic instrument panels and door panels are examples of items made using these molds. These are covers placed over many of the devices installed in front of a driver's seat, like speedometers and fuel gauges.

Since these are interior auto parts that drivers pay particular attention to, every automaker places heavy importance on them during the design phase. They are made of plastic, so if the surface stands out it will feel inorganic and downgrade what it is like to sit in the vehicle. That could downgrade the car's image. This is why KTX gives surfaces a cushioning treatment and produces a genuine leather pattern for luxury vehicles. KTX molds earn their high reputation first and foremost because they give vehicle interiors a classy feel at low costs.

Another major appeal of the molds is that they conserve energy and speed up fabrication. The conventional production process with a plastic mold is to heat it to between 300°C and 400°C, then cool it down and extract the molded product. These steps are repeated for each individual item. However, the KTX method turns this idea on its head by heating the plastic to be shaped, rather than the mold. This cuts the required energy from the usual 3,500 calories down to one-fourteenth that amount: 250 calories. It also brings fabrication time down to around 90 seconds, which is nearly one-third the time required by the normal method. Reducing both energy consumption and fabrication time is not only environmentally friendly, but also contributes directly to cost-cutting. This is why companies work zealously to shave off seconds and calories from their manufacturing processes and explains how cutting energy consumption to one-fourteenth and shortening operation time down to nearly one-third with a single stroke would earn high praise for KTX's molds.

A favor from the development phase returned

These molds were made possible by the electroforming technology and porous electroforming that KTX developed. Noda explains electroforming thus: "When plating metal or plastic, we apply a plate that is about 500 to 1,000 times thicker than normal, then use that metal plate as the mold. Most of the molds we use are made from bronze or nickel, but what we make can transcribe far more precisely than items made from molten metal poured into a cast. Depending on what is to be made, our molds may be used in work that requires nano-scale precision."

When Noda went to study in Europe, he saw something that gave him the idea that led to porous electroforming, which is now KTX's biggest seller. The auto parts factory he visited in Germany produced parts with an epoxy resin mold. To make the molded doors, the factory placed large shrinkable sheets inside a hollow space to shape it, then injected urethane inside. The resin mold had small holes in it. That was when Noda hit upon the idea of opening numerous small holes in an "electroforming mold" to enable transcription that would duplicate small bumpy patterns to make the molded product feel high-grade and more comfortable.

As soon as he got back to his company, Noda embarked upon R&D for his project. He encountered failures, such as a defective electroforming mold with 4 mm holes. But this gave him another clue that altered his thinking: "Maybe it will work if I can control the holes." His research continued for over a year, after which he succeeded in developing a mold with countless 0.1 mm holes that can process high-quality resin while conserving energy and vastly reducing operation time. He called it "porous electroforming." There was one employee who proved particularly helpful during this development process. Noda says, "We are where we are today because of his hard work."

But the mold did not receive very favorable reviews at first. The first company KTX brought it to was not interested in doing business because it had "just finished developing perforated resin molds with holes of 5 microns." President (and future Chairman) Noda and his team were not ready to give up, so they brought actual samples of items made with their mold. Although the company had previously refused to deal with KTX, this time it had just realized that its mold was not usable due to durability issues. People gradually gathered around to view the samples.

KTX also provided assistance on a daily basis, filling in holes that were too big and using lasers to widen those that were too small. The customer then decided to use the KTX concave mold. In return for this kindness, Noda secretly decided that he would allow the customer to use the molds for two years without KTX making any public announcements about their successful development. There were no contracts or memorandums exchanged whatsoever. However, KTX gathered knowledge over these two years on the number of holes required for molding, their radius, mold durability and how to handle backups. Noda says that the customer's willingness to use the new molds "helped us transition quickly to mass production. I still remember what gratitude I felt." Until the technology was patented, there was a battle among other companies in the industry to win that right. But the Japan Patent Office decided to recognize KTX as the true inventor. This competition is one of the reasons why only employees who are directly involved in mold manufacture are allowed onto the production floor.

An offensive in auto industry powerhouse America

Two years after the first company began using the new mold, KTX decided to make a push outside Japan. The first overseas market the company targeted was America, one of the world's major manufacturers of automobiles. Since KTX's patent for porous electroforming did not extend outside Japan, there was a Japanese company in the United States that was manufacturing and selling imitations. These counterfeit molds were of such inferior quality they were on an utterly different level from KTX's product, so they found very few buyers in America. But when KTX visited the big three American automakers—Ford, Chrysler and GM—they would bring out the other company's imitation, which was of similar shape, and heap scathing criticism, complaining how easily it broke and asking what KTX would do about it. Although KTX explained that its own molds were different from what this other company was producing, it could make no headway in winning over the American automakers.

The situation suddenly changed 10 years later, in 1998, when KTX received an email from a leading American automaker. To paraphrase, the email read, "When we researched interior automobile parts from around the world, we found that those in vehicles made by Japanese manufacturers were the best in terms of design, quality and other ways. Those automakers use KTX molds, so we would like you to make us a prototype." The prototype KTX delivered was well received and the American automaker decided to start using KTX's molds. This event marked KTX's serious entry into the U.S. market. The experience also led KTX to adopt a basic policy of dealing directly with overseas clients rather than going through a middleman. The company now does business with many foreign manufacturers in places like China and India and sticking to this policy has helped it deal with any problems that arise. KTX has also benefited in recent years from a lower yen.

Best in the world in seven ways

According to Chairman Noda, KTX is number one in the world in seven ways. The biggest of them is porous electroforming, while the others are normal electroforming, super porous electroforming, mesh electroforming, perforated electroforming, electroplated piping and high-precision electroforming.

Normal electroforming—generally simply referred to as "electroforming"—can produce plating 3 to 5 mm thick. As the name of super porous electroforming implies, it is a more advanced form of porous electroforming. It combines normal electroforming, laser processing and porous electroforming to perform mirror polishing and cutting. Mesh electroforming was developed to produce molded pulp products. This allows one to produce packages from recycled paper. Perforated electroforming was developed to produce molded products from polyester fibers. Greater demand is anticipated for perforated electroforming because it can be used as a carbon fiber mold to manufacture items such as aircraft parts. It can also be used to work on curved shapes that are difficult to plate. Electroplated piping goes a long way toward solving problems associated with conventional piping involving the formation and contraction of surfaces when brazed at 700°C. High-precision electroforming is used to mold backlighting in mobile phones and for high-precision mirrors. KTX has patented five of the seven technologies (the exceptions being high-precision electroforming and normal electroforming) in Germany and America, as well as in Japan.

KTX is now working on the metal piping mold (MPM) method, which heats and cools smoothly and speeds up the molding cycle. Molded products tend to bear weld marks, flow marks and sink marks on ribs and bosses, but MPM prevents these defects. In addition to making thinner molded articles and paint-less parts, two-color molds, saw material molds and foam molding, KTX has succeeded in producing light, more visually attractive parts with the MPM method. The terminology from this specialized niche market may be difficult to understand, but suffice it to say that people in the industry hold this technology in high regard. In fact, the MPM method's reputation apparently skyrocketed after it was exhibited at the International Plastics Fair (IPF) in the fall of 2014.

This is how KTX is working harder to develop new molding techniques to complement porous electroforming, the company's leading product. It is following a long-term strategy of expanding beyond automobiles and entering new growth industries like aircraft and medical instruments.

Personnel retention

When Noda was two years old, his father was killed in action in World War II. He can barely remember his face. At first he gave up on going to college so as not to burden his mother any further and instead got a scholarship to attend a local technical high school, to which he commuted from his uncle's home. Noda realized that what he'd heard from his mother—that a big company was willing to hire him through personal connection—was in fact utter nonsense when, near the end of the annual hiring season, there were only two companies still looking for people: Nagoya Rubber (now Toyoda Gosei) and Inoue Rubber (now Inoac Corporation). Noda chose to take a job at Inoue Rubber, where he worked on electroforming molds.

While employed there, Noda also attended a junior college established by a subcontractor supervised by Toyota Motor. There he learned about specialized fields like mechanical engineering and he also studied English and German. These skills not only helped him manage his company, but also proved useful in his personal life. Due to poor health, however, Noda was forced to quit Inoue Rubber. He later took a job at the Buddhist altar shop his uncle ran. He applied electroforming to produce parts for altars and one year later—it was 1965—Noda built a 50-square-meter workshop in Konan and went independent. But his business did not yield much in the way of financial results because he spent most of his time developing better electroforming methods. When business completely dried up after the oil crisis began in 1973, Noda and his employees had to get by doing odd jobs like cleaning floors at cafés. Still, Noda continued his research alone out of the desire to improve electroforming technology. This effort laid the foundation of KTX.

Mold factories were considered a dark, dirty and tough place to work. Noda had trouble retaining employees, as high school graduates would typically quit after three years at the company. In many cases, he could find no way to convince them to stay on. So he came up with the idea of a "return system" of paying wages for time away if an employee left the company but then came back to work there again. To promote better health, for new hires Noda added a 5,000-yen allowance paid to non-smokers. He also paid a 5,000-yen allowance to smokers who quit, starting the following month. When an employee had a newborn child, he provided a bonus of 300,000 yen. For lunches, Noda set up an employee cafeteria with its own chef. To encourage his workers to get married, he worked with other companies to organize parties for employees looking for a spouse. This project helped 10 or so couples tie the knot. Noda makes the company's finances transparent to all employees. When paying out bonuses, he shares easy-to-understand charts indicating earnings and expenses. Naturally, unless they have a particularly important reason, almost nobody has resigned from KTX in recent years.

Chapter 2

Specialization is the Key to Success

A Look at Five Companies:
"We Won't Go as Far as Discounting Prices Just to Make a Sale"

In this chapter, I will introduce entirely unique companies that have continued to work on refining their highly specialized technologies and manufacturing process knowhow to become world-leaders in their respective fields. Many smaller companies in Japan that were once referred to as *machi koba* (backstreet workshops) used to operate with a similar mindset to the companies I am about to introduce, but many of these workshops have now disappeared. The reasons for this include difficulties in finding fresh blood to keep the companies running and the expansion of parent companies overseas. The five companies in this chapter have stayed true to the traditional approach used by smaller Japanese companies. They provide support to Japan's manufacturing efforts while leading the world in their respective fields by fully utilizing expert craftsmanship based on masterful ingenuity and intuition.

We don't accept any bulk orders

Tokaibane Mfg. Co., Ltd. is a spring manufacturer based in Fukushima Ward, Osaka City. There are more than 3,000 spring-making companies in Japan if you count companies that also manufacture other products. Competition in the field is fierce, and companies working in it all jostle to secure as many orders as they possibly can. Unlike these other companies, however, Tokaibane declines bulk orders. "We refuse orders of 1,000 units of course, but we don't even accept orders of 100 units. We tell people who make such large orders that we don't engage in mass production and we suggest that they try ordering from another company." Despite the fact that mass-production is now the way of the world, the company continues to insist on crafting each individual spring by hand, and that makes it a truly one of a kind custom hand-made spring company. The company has no intention of changing its management policy. It is not just one of the strangest companies in Japan, but the entire world.

Springs can be found in everything from furniture to health monitors, helping us in our daily lives both behind the scenes and in plain view. The two types of springs that we use on a daily basis are "coil springs" that push back when compressed, and "extension coil springs" that support loads when extended. Tokaibane, however, manufactures a much more diverse range of springs in accordance with the various needs of its customers. These include Belleville springs that provide a large amount of power in a small space; the large springs used in railway tracks and carriages; leaf springs installed in electronic devices; ring springs that, despite having a small volume, absorb a large amount of energy; special spring-based safety mechanisms for use in dams and floodgates; and extra-powerful square springs made from materials with square cross-section profiles.

Springs for use in everything from everyday items to spacecraft and Tokyo Skytree

"Hayabusa," the asteroid probe spacecraft, was launched in May 2003 and returned safely to Earth in June 2010 with samples collected from the surface of the asteroid "Itokawa." The success of the Hayabusa mission was indicative of the high level of Japan's space-related technologies and earned acclaim from the international community. A large number of springs was used in the spacecraft including in the sampler device used to collect material from the asteroid. Tokaibane took on the job of manufacturing these springs under an exclusive arrangement. Tokaibane's springs were of course also subsequently used in Hayabusa 2.

The Japan Aerospace Exploration Agency (JAXA) developed the "Kounotori" series of cargo spacecraft to transport materials for experiments and research as well as food required by the crew of the International Space Station. Tokaibane's springs are used in the first-stage engines of HI-B rockets, which are used to launch the Kounotori spacecraft. The engines are exposed to high temperatures while passing through the atmosphere and the springs need to be able to withstand these. Tokaibane's springs were able to perform under these conditions.

When the rockets reach an altitude at which the air no longer has any impact, the payload fairing (a covering used to protect the Kounotori) is jettisoned from the rocket. When this happens, springs are used to split the payload fairing in two, and the Kounotori is then ejected from the rocket. Tokaibane also manufactured the springs used to split the payload fairing. Even when exposed in space to temperatures of approximately -200°C, the springs used to launch the Kounotori need to retain sufficient elasticity or the entire mission may end in failure. Many of the required specifications are far beyond what is ordinarily required from conventional springs, and many in the space industry were deeply concerned about whether domestic technology would be up to the task of producing springs capable of functioning under such adverse conditions. Tokaibane, however, manufactured its springs using special materials capable of performing even in space, thereby proving itself more than worthy of the trust placed in it.

At 634 meters tall, Tokyo Skytree is the world's tallest free-standing transmission tower. Rising above the 450-meter-high observatory deck on the tower, there is a narrow 140-meter-long structure called a gain tower to which broadcasting antennas are affixed. Although Tokyo Skytree is designed to withstand wind speeds that were once considered impossible based on past records, it is, in fact, normal everyday breezes that pose the most serious problems for such structures. While winds of 10 to 15 meters per second pose no problems at all at ground level, at an altitude of 600 meters they can cause serious accidents by creating a resonance phenomenon called "vortex-induced oscillation." There have been cases reported overseas where vortex-induced oscillation has been the cause of major accidents.

A device called a tuned mass damper (TMD) is installed on the top of the gain tower to prevent any such oscillations from occurring. A spring with metal fittings made by Tokaibane is used in the damper. Depending on the direction of the wind, the gain tower can be pulled away from the center line or pushed back the other way, but the damper can cope with any kind of vibration. The spring used in the damper weighs 800 kilograms. Tokaibane was selected to provide a spring for the damper because of the company's proven record in producing large springs used in high-rise buildings.

Tokaibane also manufactures springs capable of withstanding temperatures of several hundred degrees Celsius for use as components in power generation turbines in thermal and nuclear power plants. The springs protect the turbines and enable the stable supply of electricity. As you can imagine, such springs are also used at iron and steel production sites where resistance to high temperatures is required. Tokaibane's springs are also used in a variety of other fields in ways that are generally not visible but that are essential to our daily lives, including in the "Shinkai 6500" manned research submersible, and as fundamental components of the Akashi Kaikyo Bridge.

How can a company stay profitable with an average order size of only five units?

As mentioned above, Tokaibane, which manufactures springs for use in a large number of different fields, declines orders even as small as 100 units. Conversely, the company would gladly accept an order for a replacement for a single spring manufactured 10 years ago. Tokaibane is particular about crafting each and every spring by hand and the average size of the orders the company accepts is only five units. In terms of what is considered common sense in the manufacturing industry, it is unthinkable that a company that takes on such small orders could stay in business.

However, Tokaibane's sales in fiscal 2014 amounted to approximately 1.9 billion yen. Tokaibane is an extremely successful company with a gross profit of approximately 50% and an operating income of 12%. Company president Yoshiki Watanabe says Tokaibane's secret is that "customers buy our products at the prices we set." Tokaibane's mainstay customers are powerful companies such as major iron and steel producers, electric utilities and shipbuilders. Tokaibane, on the other hand, is a typical small business. Common sense in the industrial field in Japan would suggest that smaller businesses have no option but to begrudgingly comply with the demands thrust upon them by large companies. Smaller companies that are unable to withstand this are driven to either change their line of business or shut down. The fact that over the last 15 years the number of small- and medium-sized companies in Japan has dropped by more than 30% clearly indicates just how fierce the demands for price reductions from large companies really are.

Many smaller companies may find their success difficult to believe, but Tokaibane's business results prove that it's true. The company never wavers from its policy of declining large orders, even from major companies, and its stance of only taking on orders if it can expect to profit adequately. What allows the company to do this is the high level of quality it provides—which other companies are unable to replicate—and its specialization in custom-made products. There are Japanese Industrial Standards (JIS) stipulated by the Ministry of Economy, Trade and Industry that apply to springs, but Tokaibane has set its own standards which require a level of accuracy more than three times higher than that required by JIS. The company even accepts orders from individual customers in cases such as a person who has a door in which a spring has broken requiring the entire door to be replaced if nothing is done about the spring, and the company does so without cutting any corners. The majority of the springs it produces are custom-made in response to special orders from major companies, research institutes, universities and others. Therefore the prices for each spring are extremely high, from tens of thousands of yen to hundreds of thousands of yen. Herein lies the secret to the company's high profit margins.

On the other hand, the company ensures it meets delivery deadlines, and order fulfillment rate is 99.9%—almost perfect. Tokaibane began to use computers 40 years ago, before the majority of other companies. Company president Yoshiki intuitively felt that if customer information was managed using computers, it would be possible to manage information regarding when customers made their orders, what they ordered, how much they paid and so on. Now this computer-managed information can be used to immediately ascertain what kinds of springs were delivered in the past to which company and even to which individual, even if they have only ever placed a single order, and the administrative departments share this information with the manufacturing departments to allow them to respond in an effective manner immediately. The ability to accept orders based on judgments relating to production floor conditions and the number of days required to manufacture a certain spring is what allows the company to maintain an almost perfect delivery record and earn the trust of its customers.

Excess inventory isn't a waste—It's an asset

Tokaibane's greatest weapon is its dedication to craftsmanship. The process of manufacturing the handmade springs in which the company excels so much begins with the cutting of the raw material. Because of the need to have sufficient materials on hand to be able to fill orders involving different sizes and unit numbers, the company tries to maintain as large an inventory as it can. Certain special materials can end up on shelves for a year or more before being used. This is based on the company's management policy that excess inventory isn't a waste, but an asset. This runs counter to the tendency for many other companies to adopt Toyota's *Kanban* approach in which zero inventory is considered ideal. After cutting the raw material, the next step is heat molding the cut metal at temperatures of around 900°C. Judging when to remove the material from the heat is partly based on the tone of red as it glows, and this changes slightly day to day according to weather, the air temperature, humidity and other factors. This is where the experience and gut decisions of veteran employees come into play.

A robot is used during the spring-winding process. The robot is packed with craftsmanship-related knowhow, making it totally unique. Although a robot is used during this process, it is operated by veteran employees who take pride in their work as craftspeople, and the company says that this ensures that a high level of precision is maintained. Pitch adjustment is an extremely important process that determines a spring's shapes and characteristics, and adjustment down to the last millimeter is based entirely on employees' visual judgment and skills. This is truly a process in which employees fully demonstrate their skills. The types of springs which are often used inside machines need to have ends and sides that are at right angles to each other, and the ends need to be parallel with each other—these are referred to as squareness and parallelism—and a high level of precision is required. Here too, veteran employees concentrate carefully on finishing work using a machine that rotates the springs at high speed. After many different processes, the manufacturing stage comes to an end, but from here the springs are subjected to rigorous testing by inspectors who are dedicated to ensuring that not even the smallest of errors is allowed to pass them by unnoticed. The inspectors carry out a range of checks including checking the appearance, dimensions and weight of the springs as well as carrying out non-destructive analysis. These checks are implemented based on Tokaibane's own original inspection criteria and only those springs that meet these criteria are allowed to pass on to the final process of corrosion-proofing, following which they are ready for shipping. Since the company's success is so heavily dependent on the skillset maintained by its current group of employees in handcrafting the springs, it doesn't even entertain the idea of establishing overseas production bases.

The company has its own original craftsmanship exam, and employees who pass this exam are certified as expert craftspeople. The exam is apparently much more difficult than the Metal Spring Production Engineer Exam, a national examination in Japan. The company has set different levels for craftspeople from grade 1 to grade 4, and employees' wages increase as they rise from level to level. Anyone can sit the exams regardless of their age, experience and other factors, and it is not unusual at all for young employees and employees recruited from other companies to rank highly in the scoring.

In order to continue with the handcrafting approach and pass on the necessary expertise to employees even 100 years from now, the company built a special facility called Keishokan at its Toyooka Plant (in Kamiyoshidai, Toyooka City, Hyogo Prefecture). Six expert craftspeople work diligently on spring production at the facility. Working at the Keishokan is a goal for employees to aim for, and there have been employees who have cried with joy when finding out they were being assigned to the facility.

"We won't go as far as discounting prices just to make a sale"

Nowadays, Tokaibane is an entirely unique company that receives orders from around the world, but when Yoshiki assumed the role of president the company was still just a typical backstreet spring workshop. The founder, Mitsuo Minamitani, was born in a poor village in Gifu Prefecture. As a young man, he undertook an apprenticeship at a spring manufacturing company and then set up his own business. Since it was difficult as a new company without infrastructure or reputation to obtain orders from large companies, Minamitani specialized in springs that other manufacturers were reluctant to work on because they were time-consuming to produce, and he also accepted small orders. Both of his children were girls and neither of them was interested in following in their father's footsteps. Their husbands also refused to take on the role of company president. Yoshiki is the younger brother of the husband of Minamitani's second daughter. Minamitani pleaded with him to become the company president for three years until he finally caved in and took on the role. He had been told reassuring stories about how the company was profitable and that its customers were all large, trustworthy companies, but upon joining the company he found out that this was largely untrue.

Although the company wasn't in the red, it was only barely making a profit. The larger customers made unreasonable demands and orders. After being assigned to the production floor in order to learn about the work of the company, he was subjected to insidious bullying from the veteran employees, and in half a year he succumbed to *alopecia areata* (spot balding). Seeing that Yoshiki continued to focus on his work despite this, the veteran employees began to speak to him in a more polite way after a few months. He thought about quitting the company all the time, but while in Europe on an industry training trip, he heard someone say, "We won't go as far as discounting prices just in order to make a sale," and this was a revelation for him. As soon as he arrived back in Japan he implemented this approach. Customers refused to deal with the company on those terms, and there was strong resistance from inside the company as well. Yoshiki set up a project team centering on young employees to work hard on gradually implementing this new approach until it was used for every single order they received. While in Europe he also heard that employees in factories in Europe were paid well because the work they do is tough, and so he raised his employees' wages. The wages paid by Tokaibane were by far the highest in the industry. Although there were employees who quit due to personal household issues, there were no employees who quit saying they disliked the company. The company has never in its history engaged in restructuring that involved cutting jobs. When an employee's first child is born they receive a 100,000 yen gift, 200,000 yen on the birth of their second child, and amazingly enough, on the birth of their fourth child they receive one million yen. The family members of some employees pop into the company premises to have a cup of tea on their way home from shopping. The company has presumably become number one in its field because it treats its employees well.

A company that refuses to compromise on quality

TOKOSHA CO., LTD. is a typical backstreet workshop with a workforce of about 40 and an office located near Tokyo University in Bunkyo Ward, Tokyo. However, the Joewell brand of scissors that the company manufactures is favored by top hairdressers and barbers not only in Japan but around the world. The scissors are made at the company's factory in Iwate Prefecture by craftspeople who have honed their expertise over many decades and who are able to use their skill and intuition to ensure precision to within one thousandth of a millimeter. Joewell is one of the world's top brands and has sold far in excess of one million pairs of scissors.

Tokosha was established in 1917 by Toyosaku Inoue, the grandfather of the current president. The company started out as a manufacturer of medical scissors and scalpels and other such items. At the time, doctors themselves had a strong say in which medical equipment they used and this meant that sales tended to be unstable, and since the company was already making scissors for surgical use, the company began to produce scissors for barbers. Because Tokosha began producing these scissors in 1921, which happened to be the Chinese year of the rooster, the company decided to use a rooster as its trademark. Inoue was interested in the use of stainless steel as material for the company's scissors. Since surgical scissors at the time were made of iron they began to rust if subjected to steam sterilization, but stainless steel doesn't rust and Inoue felt that the way it sparkles gives a greater impression of cleanliness. One problem with stainless steel, however, is that unlike iron, it is not possible to create sharp blades with it. The company solved this problem by developing its own original technology to process stainless steel in a special way that hardens its surface. This started the company off on the road to manufacturing scissors with outstanding sharpness.

The company exhibited its new scissors at the Tokyo Peace Exhibition held in 1922 and received a silver medal. This also gave Tokosha an opportunity to increase awareness of its rooster brand. Inoue was a gifted businessman and his skills in this regard helped the company to prosper. With the start of World War II, however, the Japanese government banned men from sporting hairstyles that required cutting with scissors and pushed men to use electric hair clippers to cut their hair short. According to Toyosaku's eldest son, Hiroshi, who assumed the role of president after his father and who is currently chair of the company, "Even in times such as those, the scissors were sold secretly at high prices on the black market as haircutting scissors." The fact that black market merchants apparently used to bring in wads of cash to buy them shows just how well-regarded the scissors were in the barber industry.

During the war the military forced the company to merge with other blade manufacturers and the factory was evacuated to Nagano Prefecture. The company's own factory was restarted in 1950. Most factories had been compulsorily requisitioned for military purposes and had suffered severe damage from bombing, meaning that scissors were generally in short supply and they sold well regardless of their quality. At the time Tokosha was selling scissors with properly worked blades, so they proved extremely popular. Toyosaku, the president at the time, borrowed what was a huge sum at the time for such a small company—200,000 yen—for capital investment to increase the company's production capacity. This investment paid for itself in the first year. "In addition to our reputation from before the war, and the fact that the shortage of goods in those days meant that everything sold well, we were focused on making proper high-quality scissors that were well-received by our customers." The company has stuck steadfastly to this management philosophy of dedication to high-quality products and refusal to make or sell inferior products for more than 60 years.

"Who's bigger, Sony or you?"

Tokosha, which was a well-regarded company in Japan, came to the entire world's attention in no small part because of Vidal Sassoon, a man who is said to have brought about a revolution in the U.K.'s hairdressing industry. Sassoon was born into a poor family in London and while still young his father went missing. He struggled as he worked to polish his hairdressing skills, and in 1954 he opened his own salon. The reason he is considered to be a revolutionary by the hairdressing industry is that he brought bold changes to people's hairstyles. Until that time, women permed and set their hairstyles, but Sassoon developed unique hairstyles that didn't require perming or setting, relying on only a single pair of scissors.

As women became increasingly active in society, Sassoon's hairstyles were acclaimed by women around the world since they were suited to more active lifestyles. In this way, he took the world by storm and it is said that the hairstyles he developed are the prototypes for women's hairstyles today. This is the reason why he is even said to have changed women's lifestyles.

The only problem with Sassoon's hairstyles was that they required the use of small scissors for a proper finish. What's more, since the styles required stylists to use a single pair of scissors for long periods it placed a substantial burden not only on the scissors but also on the fingers and arms of stylists. Tokosha garnered attention because its scissors were able to withstand such use. A large number of Japanese stylists traveled to London to study Sassoon's techniques under his tutelage. Hairdressers and people aiming to become hairdressers from all around the world also went to study Sassoon's techniques, but it was the scissors made by Tokosha, which placed less burden on arms and fingers and moreover retained an outstanding level of sharpness, that began to prove popular. The teachers at the Sassoon school rated Tokosha's scissors extremely highly.

The company began exporting its scissors after buyers from the United States and elsewhere began to hear about how highly rated they were and started to visit Japan to purchase them. The company began using the brand "Joewell" after it started exporting in earnest. The brand name was based on an Anglicization of sorts of the Chinese characters used to write "Inoue," the name of the founding family. Thanks to their popularity amongst hairstylists overseas, the company launched into full-fledged exporting of the scissors in the late 1970s. The first step in the process was the setting up of a representative office in London. Exports to the United States began as a result of how highly rated the scissors were as deluxe Japanese-made products when the company exhibited them at a Beauty & Barber Supply Institute (BBSI) trade fair in Florida in 1977. At the same time that Joewell scissors were building a global reputation for themselves in the hairstyling industry, Sony was also establishing its brand in markets around the world, and according to company chair Hiroshi, "Overseas, people seriously asked us which of the two companies was larger." The company subsequently established representative offices in a range of countries and it is working to expand its sales channels not only in North America and Europe but also in Asia and Oceania.

They retain their sharpness even after a month of use

During this period when its export volumes were expanding, Tokosha was approached by a haircutting scissor company based in Solingen, Germany with a proposal to form a partnership. Solingen scissors are famous around the world, including in Japan, and are considered synonymous with the highest level of quality. However, there isn't actually a company called "Solingen." This is only the name of the city in which the scissors are made. The city thrived as a center of sword-making from the 13th century and from the 18th century craftspeople in the town began making scissors, razors and other kinds of blades. The city's manufacturers became famous for the extremely high quality of their products and rather than becoming famous as a city in which high quality blades and scissors are produced, the name of the city itself ended up becoming recognized as a sort of global brand. The city is so synonymous with high quality blades and scissors that there are Japanese blade companies that say the quality of their products is just as good as Solingen's. The proposal from the company in Solingen was described as "essentially an offer to work together on production, sales and other facets of business." What's more, the company in Solingen that approached Tokosha was a major mass producer of haircutting scissors and one of the oldest in the city.

The company was one of the most famous companies operating under the globally-recognized Solingen brand. The proposal was a fantastic opportunity with the potential to allow Tokosha to make rapid progress globally. It was not a bad offer for Tokosha at all. Inoue visited the head office of the company in Solingen and also inspected the company's manufacturing plant. It was upon visiting the plant, however, that he realized that the company used machines to mass produce its products. Although Tokosha uses machines for processes that are suited to mechanization, it carries out the important processes relating to blade sharpness, ease of use and other factors by handcrafting each individual pair of scissors. It was clear that the two companies' "manufacturing philosophies were completely different." In terms of quality as well, Inoue realized that the sharpness and ease of use of Tokosha's scissors were at a much higher level. He determined that while a partnership would have merits for the company in Solingen, there would be almost no merits for his own company, and he ultimately decided to politely decline the offer.

This particular partnership proposal was made more than 40 years ago, in the

1970s. At the time there were very few Japanese companies or industries capable of competing on an even footing against those in advanced Western nations. Tokosha was confident that its scissors were some of the best in the world, even back in those days, and this was demonstrated by the fact that, despite being a typical smaller company, Tokosha declined a partnership proposal from a company operating under the world-famous "Solingen" brand because it felt that its own products were superior. The first hairdresser in Los Angeles to start using Tokosha scissors stated that Solingen scissors lose their sharpness after a day of use, but Tokosha scissors completely retain their sharpness not only after a week, but after a full month of use. To this day, 40 years on, the company continues to rely on its manufacturing approach based on the expertise of its veteran craftspeople without resorting to mechanized mass production.

Hiroshi Kudara, who works at the factory in Iwate, is able to repair scissors to within one thousandth of a millimeter. A real veteran craftsperson who has worked in the field for 46 years, he was selected as a contemporary master craftsman and in 2013 was awarded a Medal with Yellow Ribbon. In addition, the Ministry of Education, Culture, Sports, Science, and Technology awarded Yoshiharu Chayaba and Norio Kamaishi, who also work at the same factory, with prizes for creativity for their outstanding contribution to improvements to scissor-making tools. It is not unusual for employees of smaller companies to be selected as contemporary master craftsmen or awarded with Prizes for Creativity. However, Tokosha's factory in Iwate has only 36 employees. The fact that close to 10% of the workforce has received such awards is proof of just how skilled the company's veteran employees are.

Tokosha's production of outstanding scissors begins with its procurement of raw materials. The raw materials it uses are all specially ordered from the Hitachi Metals Yasugi Works in Yasugi City, Shimane Prefecture. Shimane Prefecture is said to have prospered from ancient times by producing iron from iron sand, and Yasugi City is home to Kanayago Shrine, the main shrine dedicated to Kanayago-kami, a Shinto god of mining and iron production. Perhaps thanks to this traditional background, many outstanding manufacturers that engage in metal processing issue special orders to the Hitachi Metals Yasugi Works for raw materials. There are even machine processing companies that state emphatically that they cannot make top-quality products without raw materials sourced from the Hitachi Metals Yasugi Works. Perhaps the ancient ironmaking spirit from the earliest days of Japanese history lives on in some form in Yasugi.

Craftsmanship plus cutting-edge technology

There was a time when all of the company's processes were performed manually by craftspeople. Nowadays, processes that can be mechanized are performed by machines. Processes relating to factors that are decisive in determining the cutting performance of scissors such as the blades and screws, however, are the realm of veteran employees. The blade at the tips of scissors determines how well they cut and can therefore be said to be the most crucial part. It is apparently impossible for machines to shape blades to within one thousandth of a millimeter. Even today, the company needs to rely on the expertise of craftspeople who have decades of experience in the field. Scissor blades appear to be perfectly straight but they are in fact slightly twisted. Since the two blades are held together with a screw, the extent of the twist is one of the main factors determining the quality of scissors. In this case as well, machining to within one thousandth of a millimeter is required.

Scissors consist of two blades with handles from which power is applied by the user's fingers, and these blades are held together with a screw. One of the conditions of a good pair of scissors is that the blades, handles and screw are all aligned in a straight line. It is not possible for a machine to align these three parts in a straight line, so this has to be left up to the skills of craftspeople. If the screws are tightened too much the scissors will place an excessive burden on hairdressers' fingers. If the screws are tightened too weakly the scissors won't be able to grip the hair strongly enough, thereby undermining the cutting performance. Many of the processes that determine the cutting performance of scissors are the realm of skilled craftspeople. I have already mentioned just how much technical skill the company's craftspeople have. The eldest son of Hiroshi, the chair of Tokosha, assumed the role of president but he suddenly passed away, so Kenji, the second son of Hiroshi, took on the role. Kenji majored in engineering at university and then acquired a Ph.D. in research on scissors. "My professors were surprised, but I somehow managed to earn my Ph.D.," recalls Kenji, the current president of Tokosha. Although it's a great big world out there, it is extremely rare for someone to acquire a Ph.D. in scissor research. The fact that his father had him pursue such a Ph.D. perhaps indicates his desire to aim for yet higher levels of technology.

One form of the scissors that Tokosha has recently developed is made from an alloy that contains cobalt, a rare metal, which thus makes it safe for use for children with eczema. The company is expanding into the market for medical cutting tools in response to medical professionals who say that many tools in the field of medicine aren't user-friendly. Although much is dependent on the skills of the company's craftspeople in the field of medical tools as well, that is not necessarily all that is required in producing outstanding products.

Tokosha also needs to obtain permission to manufacture and sell medical equipment as stipulated by the Pharmaceutical and Medical Device Act (formerly under the Pharmaceutical Affairs Law). To achieve this, the company is using subsidies from the Ministry of Education, Culture, Sports, Science, and Technology, and the Ministry of Economy, Trade, and Industry to engage in collaborative R&D work with Iwate University, an institution located near the company's factories, and Chiba University. Although sales in the medical field still only account for around 10% of the company's total sales, its policy is to develop the field into one of its mainstays. Kenji, the new president, is prepared to devote himself to developing the company's business both as an engineer and as company president.

Bending pipes using a dedicated machine designed in-house

With high labor and energy costs, high corporate tax rates compared with Western nations and South Korea, and the shrinking of the domestic market as a result of depopulation, the business environment for smaller companies in Japan is certainly not good. Increasing numbers of companies are shifting production overseas. An endless stream of Japan's smaller companies, the unsung heroes that powerfully underpinned the country's manufacturing industry, are shifting to new lines of business or shutting down. It would be no exaggeration to say that the bedrock of Japan's manufacturing industry is facing a devastating crisis.

It is plain to see that a hollowing-out of smaller companies in the manufacturing industry is also occurring. Ota Ward and Shinagawa Ward in Tokyo and Higashi Osaka City used to resound to the sounds of backstreet workshop machinery and the voices of workshop employees. Walking around these areas now, you will still see such workshops still doing their best, but one can't help but feel that some of the vitality has been lost. Shops in shopping arcades in city centers all around Japan have been closing down in quick succession, leaving the arcades full of conspicuously shuttered shop fronts, and the same thing is happening to manufacturing workplaces. The current business environment makes it exceedingly difficult for small manufacturing companies to survive in Japan. Busyukogyo. CO., LTD. (Ome City, Tokyo) is a company that manufactures pipe-related automobile parts using world-leading technologies that has stood its ground in Japan, brushing aside these increasingly adverse conditions.

Busyu Kogyo suffered from a temporary worsening in its business performance, but since then its business performance has been steadily improving. The company produces metal pipes, and approximately 70% of its pipes are produced for the automotive industry, an industry considered to involve fiercer competition on price than any other. The company creates every kind of pipe used in automobiles including pipes used in engines and heat exchangers, producing on average 900 different types of pipe each month. While the company produces as many as 900,000 pipes per month on average, some of the pipes it produces are special products manufactured in small lots of several hundred units. With the company's thoroughgoing approach to high-mix, low-volume production, it is able to respond to the requirements of customers in a highly precise manner. With the trend toward reducing vehicle weights and enhancing their performance, the pipe-based components have also had to be downsized and lightened, and precision down to 0.01 millimeters is now required.

Busyu Kogyo's pipes are high-performance bent pipes manufactured by bending straight pipes in various ways. Although some of the pipes are bent 90 degrees in three or four places, the company manufactures them with micron-level (0.001 millimeters) accuracy at every bend. What's more, the company's pricing is competitive against companies in countries in which labor costs are ten to fifty times cheaper than Japan. Its reputation for technological prowess is now firmly established, as company president Hideo Hayashi explains. "I think we are probably the only company in Japan that can do what we do."

There are a large number of companies manufacturing bent pipes for use as automobile components. Many companies use abrasive machining to correct any distortion or irregularities that occur during bending work to bring their accuracy to the micron level. This machining is labor-intensive work, and is a major cost-increasing factor. Busyu Kogyo, on the other hand, manufactures pipes with micron-level accuracy without the need for any such correctional machining. The ability to manufacture products with micron-level accuracy without the need for machining is the company's biggest strength as it allows the company to compete on an equal footing with low-cost country (LCC) companies (countries from which high-precision products can be procured at the lowest price).

There is an infinite range of reasons why Busyu Kogyo is able to manufacture products in Japan at LCC prices yet with superior quality. One of these is that the company makes full use of its own original technologies to manufacture its own pipe-bending machines exclusively for its own use. Machines produced by dedicated machine tool manufacturers feature more functions, but Busyu Kogyo only uses a limited number of those functions anyway. By manufacturing its own machines in-house, the company is able to add only the functions that it actually uses. Cutting out the functions that the company doesn't require reduces the price of manufacturing the machines by more than two-thirds, and the company has also found a way to reduce power consumption by more than four-fifths. The resulting machines are compact with footprints two-thirds smaller than standard machines. There are many other benefits as well, including the fact that they can be configured in a way that makes them easier to use for employees, thereby enhancing productivity.

Gaining the consent of multitalented engineers was the key to adopting the continuous flow manufacturing method

Busyu Kogyo uses a cellular manufacturing system referred to as the continuous flow manufacturing system. With this system, everything from design to procurement of materials, production, inspection and shipping/quality management is overseen by one production supervisor. It was Henry Ford who used belt conveyor-based mass production methods to considerably reduce costs in order to produce cars that ordinary people could afford. Nowadays, not only automobile manufacturers but also many other kinds of manufacturers use this method. Limitations with the belt conveyor method were discovered, however, and recently a growing number of companies, including major electronics manufacturers, have been adopting cellular manufacturing systems, in which individual staff members oversee every process, as they come to realize the efficiency of such systems.

The fact that major manufacturing companies are now beginning to adopt cellular manufacturing methods could be seen as sufficient proof of their effectiveness. Adopting a cellular manufacturing method necessarily requires, however, that staff members are multi-skilled engineers capable of taking care of everything from materials to production and quality management, and that each such staff member has their own set of downsized production facilities. Because of this, there have been very few smaller companies that have successfully adopted cellular manufacturing methods. The main reason why Busyu Kogyo manufactures the machinery it needs in-house is that it enables the company to provide each staff member with their own set of small machines to make it possible to utilize a cellular manufacturing method. One could also say that it is the primary driver for the company's success in adopting the approach.

The company began working on fostering multi-skilled engineers in 1987, before major companies began adopting cellular manufacturing methods. At first, things didn't proceed smoothly and the company faced serious issues, but through repeated trial and error, staff members' technical skills were enhanced and now staff produce tools that suit them, and they efficiently manufacture a wide range of different product types at their own dedicated workspace. This approach improved productivity greatly and enabled the company to secure sufficient price competitiveness against China and other developing nations. It may seem simple at first glance, but continuous flow manufacturing can only succeed once a company has in place multi-skilled engineers able to take responsibility for everything from materials procurement to production management and quality management. Or rather, if a company's employees are not multi-skilled engineers, continuous flow manufacturing is completely impossible. One reason why many companies give up on the idea of cellular manufacturing methods even though they want to try them, is said to be that they are unable to foster multi-skilled engineers.

The greatest appeal of the approach is that employees can be their own "boss"

Although Busyu Kogyo does also hire university graduates, the majority of the company's employees are graduates of local technical high schools. The first thing that fresh recruits are required to master as part of their training to become multi-skilled engineers is an aluminum joining technique called *aritsuke*, which is considered to be the most difficult kind of metal welding technique there is. Although it is considered common knowledge in the industry that this technique can only be mastered by skilled workers, almost all of Busyu Kogyo's newly recruited employees are able to master the technique in one to two weeks. The company says that once they have mastered this technique, which is considered to be the most difficult, they find it easy to master the other techniques that are required of multi-skilled engineers such as electrical welding and gas welding. It is the company's unique employee education approach and working environment that makes it possible for employees to master this difficult technique so rapidly.

In addition to mastering the aluminum *aritsuke* technique, employees first of all assist established co-workers with their work through simple tasks such as cleaning components and helping with welding, and through these simple tasks they begin to learn the work that multi-skilled engineers are required to perform. They then begin to learn advanced techniques such as sheet metal, press and pipe machining.

After mastering a certain number of techniques, the employees are dispatched across a variety of different divisions to provide support. One mid-career employee told me, "Experiencing a wide range of different kinds of work taught me just how fun this work can be." On the other hand, the employee also said, "I felt that creating high-quality products through performing set groups of tasks in accordance with the rules was a rewarding experience."

The main appeal of the workplace is that, since the company uses a continuous flow manufacturing system in which each employee does all of the work and takes full responsibility for this, employees are able to work as their own boss and manage their own deadlines, quality issues and other factors. What's more, when employees are still lacking in skills and unable to produce perfect products, more experienced employees provide them with support. The company's internal education system means that employees are also able to try their hand at advanced techniques. Based on the president's idea that imposing quotas on employees is the same as imposing quotas on oneself, no quotas are imposed on work-floor employees. Employees are given the discretion as their own boss to work at a rapid pace and produce large numbers of products or work in a relaxed manner at their own pace. However, most work involves delivering products to the company that ordered them within 48 hours. This shows that this workplace in which each employee is his or her own boss still has plenty of healthy tension.

The company has a seniority system with sub-leaders, leaders, team leaders, section managers, and department managers, and each level has certain criteria that, if met, means that employees are able to earn a promotion to the next level. The first criterion is whether employees are properly performing their own work and discharging their responsibilities. For team leaders, the criterion is whether they are adequately managing their own teams. Once employees become section managers, their responsibilities suddenly become much heavier, and the criterion is whether their entire section is properly demonstrating its capabilities. The criterion for department managers is whether or not they properly take overall responsibility for their entire department. Salaries also increase as employees rise through the levels. It is an extremely clear-cut system.

These days, salaries are of course transferred electronically to employees' bank accounts for them to be withdrawn from ATMs, but company president Hayashi feels that this is too cut-and-dried and so he hands letters to every employee on pay day to thank them for their month's work. The monthly letters are currently numbered in the 220s, meaning that they have been handed out for close to 19 years now. The fact that many employees recommend the company to their friends as a satisfying and fun place to work gives an indication of Busyu Kogyo's warm and familial company culture.

We don't need a sales team

In order to establish a production system that allows the company to produce pipes and other products at prices that are competitive with LCC companies, Busyu Kogyo introduced companywide use of IT as a cost-cutting measure. The company began full-fledged use of IT six years ago, and employed engineers specialized in the field to oversee the introduction process. They worked at the factory for over a year to devise an IT system that meets the needs of the workspace and that is easy for all employees to use. The company has switched from computer terminals to iPads, which are speedy and able to display a large amount of information. Work instructions are now issued through the iPads instead of paper documents. Once a certain piece of work is completed, everything from the number of units produced that day and remaining inventory quantities to the defective product rate can be ascertained using an iPad.

Busyu Kogyo is also preparing to employ a new delivery system in which inventory information that is collated every day using iPads is communicated to customers, and customers communicate their delivery plans to Busyu Kogyo. If a customer's requirements can be met with the current inventory, Busyu Kogyo can deliver the required quantities to its customers at any time, and customers can draw up production plans with greater surety. Busyu Kogyo can also draw up production plans while at the same time monitoring its inventory, making it a system that is beneficial for both Busyu Kogyo and its customers.

Busyu Kogyo is now developing business in the field of medical care. The company is working on a disposable endoscopic surgery equipment component—a medical product that takes advantage of the company's advanced pipe technologies, which is used once in endoscopic surgery on internal organs and is then disposed of. Endoscopic instruments were developed in Japan, and Japan also has an overwhelming market share, so Busyu Kogyo has high expectations regarding prospective demand in the field for its product. Busyu Kogyo has not relied on sales promotions to grow its business. Instead it has built up its reputation as a company that manufactures outstanding pipes and has world-leading pipe-bending technology. Furthermore, the company aims to meet the needs of customers who place orders based on its reputation, using its advanced technologies. For this reason the company has had no need for a sales team. As a result of management focused on meeting customer needs, Busyu Kogyo shifted in the direction of high-mix, low-volume production.

The company's move into the field of medical care came about in a similar manner. A customer who had heard about the company's reputation for possessing world-leading pipe production technologies went to Busyu Kogyo with a proposal. By continuing to meet the requirements of medical equipment manufacturers by providing them with high-quality components, the company's business in the field has grown and now accounts for close to 30% of the company's sales. The medical field is an industry of the future, and further sales increases are to be expected. Busyu Kogyo has no intention of changing its management policy of being a domestic company, and focusing on high-mix, low-volume production with particular attention paid to cost and quality.

Conquering the world with "mother machines"

Homma Machinery Co., Ltd. (Yodogawa Ward, Osaka City) specializes in manufacturing large-scale machine tools. With capital of 49 million yen and a workforce of 140, the company is certainly not a large one, but its machine tools are used to manufacture all of the wheels of Shinkansen trains, which operate on high-speed railway systems that are acclaimed internationally as the world's safest. Switch rails, or crossing rails, which are used at railway points, are also manufactured using the company's specially devised machine tools.

The company's machine tools helped to considerably increase the speed of Shinkansen trains. The company's machine tools have also been used to carry out machining where an accuracy of one micron (0.001 mm) is required. Such machining has been carried out on Tokyo Skytree's elevators, pressure vessels used in nuclear power plants and other items. With its specialized machine tools the company has established its position as a unique company, and "Homma" is now a global brand.

Modern life would simply be impossible without machines. No matter what field they operate in, be it the automotive or electronics field or any other field, it would be impossible for manufacturers to produce products without machines. It's no exaggeration to say that machines underpin modern lifestyles. "Machine tools" are a type of machine used to create a diverse range of different components by subjecting various kinds of metals to a range of machining processes such as piercing, grinding and polishing. Machine tools are used to manufacture the components used in everything from precision devices such as cameras and clocks to large products such as aircraft, high-speed trains, automobiles and ships. Components manufactured using machine tools are assembled to produce automobiles, consumer electronics, etc. One of the determining factors in the performance of these products is the precision with which the components are manufactured using machine tools.

Since they are machines that manufacture machines, machine tools are also referred to as "mother machines." Machine tools have evolved in step with industrial development and a range of different kinds has now been developed to meet a wide variety of needs. Their sizes range from small units that can be easily transported by hand to machines that are as large as buildings. Homma Machinery excels at manufacturing the latter—large and extra-large machine tools—and the company has an overwhelming market share in this field.

One example of work performed using Homma's machines is the machining of large metal components for use in the Akashi Kaikyo Bridge. The 3,911-meter-long bridge, which links the City of Kobe to Awaji Island, is registered in the Guinness World Records as the world's longest suspension bridge, with a central span of 1,991 meters. The main cables from which suspension bridges are suspended could be said to be the most crucial part of suspension bridge structures. The towers used to suspend the main cables of the Akaishi Kaikyo Bridge rise 300 meters above the surface of the sea. The bases of the towers were made by stacking up 450-ton metal blocks followed by slightly lighter metal blocks. A total of 30 such blocks were used in each tower and the deviation at the tops of the towers had to be kept roughly within two centimeters. If not, the safety of the bridge would be compromised. The method used to achieve this involved placing 450-ton blocks at the base and stacking 300-ton blocks on top of these. The surfaces of these blocks that come into contact with other blocks had to be processed with micron-level accuracy. Homma's five-axis facing machine was used for this processing work, and the machine slashed processing time to a fifteenth of what it conventionally would have taken.

Just how outstanding Homma Machinery's technological capabilities are is clearly shown by one of its multifunctional machine tools, referred to as a five-surface processing machine. This machine is similar to a massively enlarged machining center and is capable of carrying out a wide range of machining on five surfaces of a six-faced object (the base of the object is not machined) including planing, grooving, piercing, threading, etc. The machine makes it possible to perform the work of more than two conventional machines at once. Homma Machinery manufactures two different types of five-surface processing machines: One with a table that can be moved backwards and forwards, and one with a gantry that can be moved backwards and forwards (the latter is more technologically difficult to manufacture).

The company also produces a machine tool called a "turn miller," which is a combination of the abovementioned five-surface processing machine (with a moving gantry), and a large vertical "turning center" (a machine tool used to process rounded objects). The production of turning centers, which are composite machine tools that use vertical lathes with revolving tools to provide more advanced functionality, requires extremely advanced technological capabilities.

These turn millers are used to process components used in, amongst other things, the pressure vessels that sit at the heart of nuclear power plants. Large pressure vessels (for use in gigawatt-class nuclear power plants) measure 8 meters in diameter and 22 meters in height, and even small pressure vessels are massive devices measuring roughly 4.4 meters in diameter and 13 meters in height. To ensure a high level of safety for these supersized pressure vessels, ultraprecise micron-level processing of surface deviations is required. If you consider the size of the vessels and the fact that one micron is 0.001 millimeters, you will realize that such processing requires a level of accuracy that is close to nanometer-level (0.000001 millimeter) machining, which is considered to be at the extreme cutting edge of technology. Public sentiment in Japan is now strong against nuclear power generation, making construction of new facilities in Japan difficult. Since demand for nuclear power remains strong in China, Southeast Asia, the Middle East and elsewhere, Homma's large turn millers are highly likely to continue to be used around the world.

The demand in Japan for spent nuclear fuel storage vessels (metal casks), however, is forecast to grow. Homma's large turn millers are also used to process components used in these storage vessels. Although the fuel they contain is spent, a high level of impermeability is required to ensure that no radiation can leak from them.

Homma's machines have even contributed to the discovery of old documents inside Buddhist statues

Japan used to produce so many ships that people said it ruled the seven seas. As a result of this historical background, there is still quite a large number of Japanese industries and companies with leading global market shares in the field of shipbuilding-related machines. Even today, Japan still has the top global share in the engine crankshafts used in large ships, and it is Homma's large machine tools that underpin their production. Crankshafts can reach lengths in excess of 25 meters. They are manufactured by joining together metal parts each measuring several meters in length, and it is said that Homma's machine tools are simply the best for manufacturing components used to join such parts, whether they be large or small.

The elevators installed in Tokyo Skytree, a popular sightseeing spot, are famous for their high speed. Homma's machine tools were also used to manufacture many of the rails installed in the elevator shafts of Tokyo Skytree to enable emergency stops if there is a sudden earthquake, change in the weather, or other such incident. The technological capacity to manufacture these rails with an accuracy within 0.001 millimeters is a matter of life or death.

Homma Machinery also manufactures products that are utilized unseen behind the scenes to protect people's lives, such as the main body of medical devices used to treat cancer with protons. Homma also manufactures the main body of CT scanners that were used to inspect H-II rocket fuel tank boosters. The company also manufactures smaller CT scan devices that have also been used to inspect old swords and Buddhist statues, and it is thanks to this device that old documents were discovered inside a Buddhist statue. "We were focused on manufacturing large machine tools that provide a high level of accuracy, but the scope of our work has expanded. Before we knew it, we weren't only producing general-use large machine tools but also responding to orders for machines used in everything from nuclear power to cutting-edge medicine," says company president Yoshiro Homma. What makes the company different from other machine tool manufacturers is that almost all of its products are manufactured in response to special one-off orders.

Normal machine tool manufacturers have salespeople who travel around visiting potential customers with pamphlets and prototypes. In the case of Homma Machinery, however, the company only begins working on a machine once it has ascertained what it is a customer requires. The company begins negotiations by listening to the customer's requirements and then moves on to the design work. In many cases, customers approach the company because their orders were rejected by other manufacturers who were unable to produce what was required, or alternatively, because they expect right from the start that only Homma Machinery would be able to produce what they require. Almost all of the orders the company receives are for large or extra-large precision machines or for machines with functions that have conventionally been considered impossible. The company has always worked to meet the requirements of orders like these carefully one at a time.

Technology underpinning the speed of Shinkansen super-express trains

The best proof of just how precise Homma's machine tools are, and just how well-trusted by customers the company is, is the abovementioned fact that 100% of Shinkansen train wheels are manufactured using the company's machine tools. Shinkansen trains travel at over 300 kilometers per hour. Moreover, they are operated at intervals of only several minutes. The density of their timetables rivals those of commuter train services in large cities. Despite this, however, there have been no major accidents involving Shinkansen since their launch. Because of this, Shinkansen services have earned praise from people in the railway industry around the world. Strict safety criteria have been established for all aspects of services and only Homma's machine tools are capable of manufacturing Shinkansen wheels, one of the most important components of Shinkansen trains. The wheels are 860 mm in diameter and weigh 300 kg. They are grinded and machined with an accuracy of 0.001 mm. The roundness of the wheels, which determines their balance quality, also requires similar precision machining. 100% of wheels on ordinary non-Shinkansen trains in

One of Homma Machinery's machine tools for crossing rail machining

Japan are also manufactured using Homma's vertical machine tools.

The company's machine tools used for manufacturing railway crossing rails (used at track switching points) are considered to be the best not only in Japan but in the world. Since replacing crossing rails after they have been installed is an arduous task, they are made from a special type of steel material with large amounts of manganese that can be used for much longer than ordinary railway tracks. In addition to being extremely hard, the surface of the material hardens during machining meaning that grinding work can only be carried out once. If the first attempt isn't successful, it is not possible to start over partway through. It is said that only Homma has the technological capabilities required. It is also said that ever since Homma's machine tools became capable of manufacturing crossing rails exactly in line with ideal shapes identified through computer analysis, the speed of Shinkansen trains has increased markedly. Although Shinkansen motors, carriages and other items are conglomerations of cutting-edge technologies, and speed increases haven't only been due to Homma's crossing rail machine tools, there can be no doubt that the company's machine tools have made a significant contribution in this regard.

Essentially an entirely unique company

Homma's greatest strength is that it takes care of not only development and design, but also everything from the cutting and welding of necessary parts, to machine processing and final assembly, and the company does all this at its own factory facilities. Since almost all of the machines used at the processing plant are also manufactured in-house, it goes without saying that if any glitches are detected they can be rectified immediately. As a result, it is possible for the company to streamline work processes and enhance the precision of the products it manufactures. The fact that the company manufactures what it requires in-house rather than purchasing from other companies, "ultimately means that we are also enhancing our own technologies," says Homma. When manufacturing a large machine tool, first of all it is necessary to create the basic structure through a process called "plate working" that requires complex and advanced skills involving cutting metal plates and welding them together. Many machine tool manufacturers purchase such structures readymade or outsource their production because they think it is too troublesome and costly to do in-house. Homma however, has created its own plate working plant within one of its factories. This is because the company is particular about taking responsibility for the production of its machines throughout the manufacturing process.

Plate working is carried out by veteran employees with extremely advanced welding skills who have honed their techniques for decades in the welding department. There are also younger employees in the welding department who learn welding techniques from these veteran employees and who will make up the next generation of veterans. This is the approach taken not only in the welding department but in every other department as well. Homma has delivered nearly 600 machines to customers overseas in over 30 different countries. Despite the company's prices being 30% to 40% higher than those of competitors, it is not unusual for companies to approach Homma with proposals first of all, and recognition of the Homma brand is beginning to grow within the global machine tool industry.

Homma was established by Yoshiro's grandfather as a cast iron foundry called Homma Cast Iron Works in 1946 immediately after WWII. When the second president (Yoshiro's father Hirokazu) manufactured a large machine to process cast iron products in-house, one of Homma's major customers saw the machine and placed an order, and the company began manufacturing large machine tools from that point. "Machine tool manufacturers generally start off producing small machine tools and then progress to larger ones, but we manufactured large machine tools right from the start," says company president Yoshiro Homma. While it was the second president Hirokazu who laid the foundations for Homma Machinery to become the company it is today, it was the current president, Yoshiro, who has navigated successfully through the "lost 20 years" following the collapse of Japan's bubble economy and who developed Homma into a technologically advanced company.

Yoshiro became the company's fifth president in 1998. At the time, Japan was facing an economic slowdown so serious that even leading commercial banks were going bankrupt. The machine tools industry is said to be the industry most affected by changes in economic conditions, and even major well-established machine tool manufacturers began to incur massive losses. In addition, management missteps by the third and fourth presidents meant the company ended up facing such severe business conditions and cash-flow problems that it was struggling to make ends meet month to month. Despite these conditions, however, Homma managed to turn its business around by specializing in the area it excelled in: Producing large high-performance machine tools. By 2008 Homma's business performance had fully recovered, and the company marked this fresh start by changing its name to Homma Machinery Co. Ltd.

Even after the post-bubble economic slowdown, established machine tools manufacturers continued to go out of business, and major machine tools manufacturers downsized, leaving Homma in an entirely unique position as a self-reliant manufacturer specializing in large machine tools. The company is not resting on its laurels, however, and is looking to the future in developing its business.

A company with such a high level of integrity it is trusted to print banknotes

The head office and factory of YASDA PRECISION TOOLS K.K. are located in Satosho, a small town in Asakuchi District, Okayama Prefecture, 40 minutes on the Sanyo Main Line from Okayama's Shinkansen station. The site is surrounded by farmland, and such is the natural beauty of the area it would make businesspeople who live amid the hustle and bustle of large cities think, "If only I could spend the rest of my working career in an environment like this...."

The company manufactures machine tools with micron-level (0.001mm) accuracy. Many of its machine tools are manufactured with not only micron-level accuracy but submicron-level (0.1 micron) accuracy. Japan is one of the top producers of machine tools, but even amongst Japan's various machine tools companies, Yasda Precision Tools is a company that specializes in manufacturing machine tools that truly deserve to be designated as ultraprecision tools, and world-famous companies line up to place orders with the company. The fact that the company's machine tools have been used in the production of Ferrari Formula One vehicle engines probably proves just how technologically advanced they are.

Japan became a global standard machine tools manufacturing country in the 1980s, and Japanese companies still maintain a market share of approximately 22%; roughly the same as those in Germany. It is only a roughly one trillion-yen market, however, and with nearly 100 companies competing, competition is fierce. Just how heavily the machine tools industry is affected by economic conditions is shown by the fact that the number of orders received during the 2008 global financial crisis dropped by two-thirds. As mentioned above, the field is so merciless and so vulnerable to the vicissitudes of economic fluctuations that even major machine tools companies are driven to bankruptcy.

As a result of these conditions, there is a trend for smaller machine tool manufacturers to specialize in certain areas such as ultraprecision machine tools requiring submicron-level accuracy for use in cutting-edge manufacturing, or large machine tools used to manufacture components for ships, aircraft, steam turbines for use in electricity generation plants and other items. Yasda Precision Tools has opted for the former. I provided the example above of Homma Machinery, which is a modestly sized company that is a world-leader in the field of large machine tools, but the machine tools that Yasda Precision Tools produces are ultraprecision machine tools that have taken the world by storm.

If one compares Japan's banknotes to those of the United States or China it is strikingly obvious that Japan's banknotes are printed in a much more sophisticated way than those of other countries. Chinese hotels place 100 yuan banknotes in a machine to count them but it is said that one reason for this is to identify counterfeit notes. There was also an incident in which large numbers of counterfeit 100 US dollar notes were discovered in Southeast Asia. No incident involving large numbers of Japanese banknotes has occurred, however. All of Japan's banknotes are printed by the National Printing Bureau. It is said that the technology used to create the watermarks, and print subtle and elaborate details such as whiskers and hair is so advanced that it cannot be easily replicated overseas. The printers used to print Japan's banknotes are manufactured by a major printing machine manufacturer with a factory in Ibaraki Prefecture. Yasda Precision Tools manufactures an extremely important component of these printers that prevents positional aberrations from occurring.

Although Japanese watchmakers are well-regarded around the world for their advanced technological capabilities, Swiss watches still have stronger brand power and are considered to be synonymous with luxury watchmaking. Yasda Precision Tools also produces machine tools used by major Swiss watchmakers to manufacture watch components. Since watches themselves are ultraprecision machines, it goes without saying that the components used in them need to be manufactured with nanometer-level accuracy. What's more, Yasda Precision Tools competed with local Swiss companies for the contract in question, and won because the excellence of the company's machine tools was ultimately recognized.

The performance of smartphones has rapidly improved to the extent they are no longer simply mobile telephones but information devices that allow users to enjoy games, music and even videos. To create the external structure of smartphones, metallic molds are required. Since they are equipped with camera lenses requiring micron-level accuracy, it goes without saying that the metal molds need to be manufactured with at least the same precision.

Even metal molds for shampoo containers require a very high level of accuracy, despite the fact that at first glance they don't appear to. Since the containers are produced in batches of 80 to 100, any slight deviation or discrepancy in accuracy is unthinkable. Yasda Precision Tools also produces the machines used to produce such ultraprecise metal molds.

When it comes to machines such as aircraft and automobiles, the accuracy with which they are manufactured can be a matter of life or death. Only companies that receive special accreditation are allowed to produce aircraft components. Yasda Precision Tools' machine tools are used to manufacture components for the major U.S. aircraft manufacturer Boeing. The company's machine tools are also used to manufacture Formula One race car engines. Formula One races are considered to be the most fiercely contested car races of all and the automakers that participate build their race cars from scratch, especially staking their pride and honor on how well they fare. As mentioned above, Yasda Precision Tools' machine tools have also been used to produce engines for Ferrari, a company that many car fans around the world are infatuated with. "Our machines being used by Ferrari provided us with a great opportunity to establish our position within the industry," says company president Takuto Yasuda. The company has also supplied a major German automaker with machines for use in machining race car engines.

Innovations aimed at enhancing precision

One meter of steel, the raw material of machine tools, expands 10 microns when its temperature increases by one degree Celsius. Almost all machine tools are manufactured from steel so if there is any variation in the temperature of the factories in which they are assembled, deviations would arise. The company uses a factory that can be kept at a certain temperature throughout the facility to prevent this. Sensors are installed at one-meter intervals and the system is designed to not only keep the factory as a whole at a constant temperature but also automatically rectify any variations of over one degree Celsius that may occur in any particular part of the facility. A constant temperature can be maintained inside such factories, from the floors right up to the ceilings that are three to four times higher than the tops of the large machine tools, regardless of whether it is a scorching hot summer day or a subzero day in the middle of winter.

The company's first constant temperature factory, which was constructed about 30 years ago, had no windows. This was because sunlight shining directly on the machinery would cause slight variations in precision levels. The development of heat-blocking glass and consideration for the feelings of employees led the company to add windows to its third factory, which was completed recently and has windows situated on the north side which receives no direct sunlight. "The reason why we are so particular about this, is that if steel pieces that have been grinded to match with micron precision, end up expanding or contracting by a few microns or even less than that, at the assembly plant, the precision of the resulting machines will be impacted and we need to prevent that from happening," says production department manager Yoji Tanabe.

This is not the only innovation aimed at enhancing the precision of the company's machines. People generally consider iron and steel to be rigid materials that do not deform. Yasda Precision Tools, however, views iron as something that is soft and that changes shape. Even machine tools made from a rigid material like steel will deform, albeit only slightly, when superstructures weighing hundreds of kilograms and in some cases thousands of kilograms are placed on them. Yasda Precision Tools adjusts machine tools with micron-level precision to ensure that their shape after such deformation occurs will be ideal. The company takes into account measurements of micron-level deformations in steel resulting from particular weight loads.

A work process called hand scraping, which used to be carried out at all machine production plants, is still carried out at Yasda Precision Tools. The work involves using a tool called a hand scraper consisting of a blade made from steel and other materials usually with a 30 cm to 40 cm wooden handle. After clearly marking out where the protrusions and depressions are on the material to be worked, the blade is used to scrape the surface of the material. The skilled engineers who use these tools customize them in their own unique ways to make them easier to use, and daily maintenance of the blade is an important aspect of the work.

When the company's employees carry out hand scraping, the material to be worked is painted with vermilion paint, and the surface of the material is rubbed against another flat surface. The paint gets rubbed off any parts of the material that are protruding, and these parts are scraped down by hand. The employees place their body weight on their hand scrapers—which they grow very fond of—and scrape off one or two microns of material from the surface. They repeat this process over and over to give the material a perfectly precise surface flatness. It is said that mastery of the techniques involved takes five years, and to be able to properly apply the process to all kinds of materials takes a further five years. Companies that place more emphasis on cost than performance would of course switch to a mechanized version of this process. Yasda Precision Tools, however, is able to maintain its high level of precision through the use of hand scraping and is so particular about it that it even says, "The day we stop using hand scraping will be the day Yasda Precision Tools ceases to exist."

The company has plenty of young skilled workers working night and day to achieve their aim of becoming hand scraping engineers.

High precision machines are made from high precision components

Yasda Precision Tools' factory has a large number of machines, including a state of the art machining center that can be used to perform several different tasks simultaneously. In line with its management philosophy—"High precision machines are made from high precision components"—the company manufactures the machines themselves. Information about even the most trivial events that occur during the performance of daily tasks is fed back to each department, and this information is utilized in the enhancement of work processes and development of new products. Once components have been processed in the factory, they are subjected to stringent submicron-level measurements to ensure they meet the required precision levels. The room in which the components are measured is kept at a constant temperature to prevent temperature changes from having an impact on the precision of the measurement equipment and the components to be measured. If necessary, the components are subjected to hand working before undergoing a submicron-level product inspection, and only products that pass this inspection are delivered to customers. The fact that the company has an extremely large number of repeat customers is presumably due to efforts such as these.

Yasda Precision Tools' brand is already well-established in Japan, and the company is receiving an increasing number of orders from famous overseas companies. The company believes that it is sales to overseas companies that will experience further growth. The company has established a base in Germany and a subsidiary in Shanghai, China. Thus far, the company has dispatched employees overseas to provide after-service, but from now on it cannot expect to expand sales through the provision of more thoroughgoing services to its overseas customers.

Yasda Precision Tools was established in Osaka by Shinjiro Yasuda, grandfather of the current company president Takuto Yasuda. Initially, the company was a factory with a workforce of three that bored automobile engine cylinders. The three periods in which the company developed most were the cylinder boring period, the early machining center period, and the period in which the company developed high-precision machining centers. Aiming to make not the largest machine tools but the best, Shinjiro, the company's founder, purchased a cutting-edge machine tool from a major U.S. machine tools manufacturer. The machine tools were so expensive that the company's bank was reluctant to finance the purchase. Based on the purchased machine tool, the company successfully developed a milling machine with an extremely high level of precision, and this laid the foundations for the company's subsequent shift toward becoming an ultraprecision machine tools manufacturer.

The company subsequently developed a machining center in the latter half of the 1960s and its business began to expand rapidly. By the early 1980s, the company's technology had advanced so much that it licensed machining center technologies to a manufacturer in the United Kingdom. The post-war economic boom that Japan was enjoying at the time also served to underpin Yasda Precision Tools' development. The company released a string of new products onto the market in response to market requirements, and its sales steadily grew. With the collapse of the bubble economy, however, the company's sales decreased dramatically. The company was hardly able to sell any of its newly developed machines at all.

Since, in accordance with its management policy that employees were its greatest resource, the company didn't make any redundancies, forcing the company to struggle through a long and painful period. "This put the company in the toughest position it had faced since its founding," said company president Takuto Yasuda. In the midst of these difficulties, the company received an order for a machine tool for manufacturing metal molds. Although the company had no knowledge at all relating to machine tools for metal molds, it worked together with the customer and by applying the technologies it has accumulated the company was able to reduce production time considerably while also greatly enhancing precision levels. Today, machine tools for metal molds are one of the company's bread-and-butter products providing a supporting foundation and accounting for nearly half of the company's sales. The machine tools market is roughly divided into two segments: one centered on mass-produced general-purpose products targeted at a large number of customers, and a much smaller one centered on high-precision products. When a company pursues higher levels of precision, its market will contract. For this reason, the machine tools market is considered to be pyramid-shaped.

Mass-producing manufacturers target the large market at the bottom of the pyramid. This is because as greater precision is pursued as you move up the pyramid, the market grows smaller. If you follow the management philosophy of Yasda Precision Tools—making not the largest machine tools but the best—you will head toward the peak of the pyramid, and a smaller market.

Although the market does grow smaller, each time the company raises its technologies to the next level, the number of its competitors also decreases. There is another virtuous cycle as well: The more its reputation grows, the less likely the company is to be dragged into competition on price.

The company indicates that it intends to expend even greater effort in extending its technological capabilities yet further, saying, "We have managed to grow our business this far because of the high precision and functionality of our products. This is one of the reasons why we will therefore continue to be very particular about aspects relating to precision and performance." The company is going to continue to make its way up to the apex of the machine tools pyramid with ultraprecision machine tools that are the first choice of its customers.

Chapter 3

Four Companies Taking on the World with Highly-Advanced Technologies

Undaunted by Domestic Harassment

Japan is considered to be a world leader in nano-tech and other highly-advanced technologies. Major corporations with their huge pools of talented engineers and wealth of development capital occupy predominant positions at the heart of these technologies. Japan's strength in these technologies, however, can be found in its many small and medium-sized enterprises (SMEs) with world-leading, highly-advanced technologies on par with major corporations. While their names may not always be known to those outside of researchers and experts because of their high specialization, the existence of such SMEs with highly-advanced technologies underpins Japan's competitive strengths in automobiles, robotics and other fields. These SMEs also play a role as important support for future industries such as linear motors, aviation, space and advanced medicine, among others, which means they even represent the key for the future development of Japan's economy as a whole.

Coming to grips with half-formed research aims

KITANO SEIKI CO., LTD. employs a workforce of 28 and has paid-in capital of 15.44 million yen, making it a typical small-scale backstreet workshop. It makes testing equipment. However, Kitano Seiki's products are not your ordinary testing equipment. Japan has many researchers who could very well win a Nobel Prize in the fields of chemistry, physics and others. Kitano Seiki excels at ultra-high-tech testing equipment used in extremely advanced research and development and the next Nobel

Prize winner from Japan might just be a researcher using Kitano Seiki's testing equipment. Kitano Seiki was also involved in the basic research on linear motors, which is a field where Japan is attempting to be a world pioneer. Its ability to create research and development systems with highly-advanced technologies means Kitano Seiki has world-leading technologies. Tokyo's Ota Ward, where it is headquartered, was once a region with a high concentration of Japan's leading manufacturing SMEs. However, the number of these companies has been cut to less than half of its peak, which was caused by major corporations relocating production bases offshore. Nevertheless, in defiance of such a harsh environment, the company continues to humbly manufacture testing equipment that meets the needs of researchers looking to engage in world-leading research and development.

Kitano Seiki's greatest trait is that nearly all of its products are unique, specially-ordered items best described as "creating more than a thousand one-of-a-kind products for researchers." Because it concludes confidentiality agreements when making products for private sector companies, the general public is largely not aware of how Kitano Seiki creates its products and where its products are being used. However, most of its products are fabricated at an extremely-high level that cannot be replicated by other companies. There are a large number of companies in Japan, both big and small, that make testing equipment, such as Shimadzu Corporation, a company with its own Nobel Prize winning researcher, but despite this number, most have thrown in the towel when it comes to making the difficult testing equipment that Kitano Seiki produces. For this reason, there are countless cases where people head to Kitano Seiki as a last resort. In the process, Kitano Seiki has created numerous excellent products that have fully satisfied the needs of its customers.

Kitano Seiki's sales and marketing efforts begin with staff trying to come to grips with a particular researcher's half-formed research aims. Researchers create new substances that are the first of their kind in the world and conduct research that fundamentally challenges established scientific theories. Kitano Seiki helps make this possible by holding meetings with researchers at a stage when they have just developed a vague idea about trying to prove a revolutionary theory that no one else has ever considered and are still thinking about how to go about doing so. Because at this stage the researchers' thoughts have yet to be properly organized, they do not have a clear idea of what type of equipment they can use to get the results they need, nor how to use such equipment even if they did. Kitano Seiki receives requests from researchers with ideas that are not yet fully formed. Based on this, the company comes up with a proposal and discusses it in detail with the researchers and through this process it is able to give tangible form to the researchers' vague ideas. Kitano Seiki then begins to make arrangements for the basic design of the testing equipment.

Once several meetings are held to present solutions and the final okay is given by the researchers, Kitano Seiki then enters the design and development stage. The company has employees who just need to borrow a desk in the researchers' laboratories or head to a nearby café to immediately put together a basic schematic diagram in around two to three hours. Only a few of Kitano Seiki's employees have such advanced engineering abilities to do this, but the rest of the company's employees can put together a basic schematic diagram in around two to three days after they have met several times with a researcher and obtained approval for their proposal.

Kitano Seiki's employees include those who have a fundamental love of machinery, who learned machining from high school to college, aiming to eventually work in manufacturing using machinery, and who looked at many companies and decided to join Kitano Seiki after falling in love with its approach to manufacturing where each and every product is custom made. There are also employees with strong ambition, who are from machining families and who wanted to work for a company that creates things from scratch, unlike major corporations that only mass produce parts using assembly-line production systems, and so decided to join Kitano Seiki to do what they love.

In most cases, work begins by creating the parts for testing equipment because this equipment is the first and therefore obviously the only one of its kind in the world. Although some of these parts are created in-house, most are made by small factories like Kitano Seiki located mainly in Tokyo's Ota Ward. Although their past prosperity is no longer evident today, the neighborhoods around Ota Ward are filled with leading small, backstreet workshops. Even today, small family-owned companies with only two or three employees still exist and a tradition still lives on where these small companies cooperate with one another. Using this network, anyone can obtain high quality components. There are also still SMEs and micro-sized enterprises that have the craftsmanship to accommodate the rather impossible order of having a part delivered the next day with excellent precision and quality.

Once the parts are completed, the process moves on to assembly. Each individual part is assembled and connections are welded. Most of this work relies on manual dexterity developed over many years through experience and intuition. Among this work, some processes involve perseverance and tedious work, assembling several times in order to make changes on the micron level. However, the employees involved in this work say it is interesting because they have to constantly innovate and devise new approaches.

Kitano Seiki differs from ordinary manufacturers because of its thorough fixation on the design of test equipment. This fixation is based on the company's philosophy: "Researchers do not like poorly designed equipment, regardless of how many functions it may have, and such equipment could have a detrimental impact on the research laboratory or office where it is installed. The lack of a positive environment could affect research outcomes." Additionally, Kitano Seiki designs its machinery while giving consideration to the size of the research lab or office and where it will be installed. Some of its most advanced testing equipment is shaped like robots out of a science fiction movie and are packed tightly with precision instruments. The hidden machinery that connects to the testing equipment is designed flawlessly, while the ultra-precision instruments used to develop advanced technologies and instruments for automatically recording results are impeccably packed inside. It is not uncommon for researchers to say "just looking at Kitano Seiki's testing equipment whets my appetite for research," which indicates that researchers are won over from the moment they see the design and all of the cutting edge technologies found inside.

Once the test equipment is completed, a quality inspection is performed to make sure it fits the design diagram. The completed test equipment requires a level of precision that is nearly always ultra-precise, because some require testing on a nano-meter (meaning a millionth of a millimeter) scale, or at absolute zero or temperatures close to it at extreme low temperature environments close to -273.15°C, which are considered to be scientifically impossible. As such, work in the production process is carefully carried out all the way down to single small components. At Kitano Seiki, veteran employees who have worked there for decades and are considered masters of their craft, as well as younger employees attempting to learn the ropes of the technologies work carefully through diligent application. It is only natural to check whether the overall functions fully clear the requirements of the customer. Kitano Seiki's employees inspect, in ultra-fine detail, the parts that were used and whether calibrations and functions are working according to design diagrams. This makes the work very delicate, so much so that it is a "battle" between the equipment and the engineers who complete it.

Aiming to be a company that not only competes but also creates

Once the testing equipment is completed, it is time for installation. According to the group leader of the company's Sales Engineering Department, on-time delivery and ensuring equipment functions per specification are a matter of course because "Kitano Seiki's customers are researchers on the leading edge internationally, so being a day late, or lacking the required specifications or functions can potentially cause significant losses to these researchers." The other thing that customers require is for equipment to be installed as soon as it is delivered so they can start research. Installation work requires nerves of steel as even the slightest measurement error or deviation caused by the smallest amount of clumsiness or mistake cannot be tolerated because of the precise nature of the testing equipment. "Ideally, equipment with greater than expected functions can be created and delivered in one shot," and the entire company works hard toward this goal. If the equipment does not fulfill the expected functions or a deficiency is found due to the slightest trouble from installation, calibration and adjustments are continually made until the promised functions are delivered. On occasion, the testing equipment needs to be disassembled for further inspection or modification.

Another unique trait of Kitano Seiki is its after-sales services. If more advanced testing is required due to advancements in science and technology, Kitano Seiki will send out engineering staff at the request of the customer to make repairs and modifications to equipment that has already been delivered. Kitano Seiki accepts such requests even for equipment made by other companies and there are several cases to date where it has greatly boosted the capacity of another company's equipment successfully by making modifications. Kitano Seiki also carries out regular maintenance on its equipment and units after delivery. Once a certain period of time passes, no matter how excellent the equipment may be it will experience a decline in its functions. Such equipment is taken back to Kitano Seiki's factory where it is overhauled and restored to the same performance it offered at the time of delivery. If a testing facility or research lab relocates, Kitano Seiki will assist with the relocation work. Sometimes this involves moving the testing equipment all in one piece, while other times Kitano Seiki may have to disassemble, box, ship, deliver and re-install it.

Kitano Seiki aims to be an organization that offers a family environment where employees not only compete but also create. Kitano Seiki's motto is summarized as follows: "Competition results in losers, but competition and creation and co-creation always results in winners. People will grow remarkably together by combining their talents and creating while also bringing their fresh ideas and creativity to the table for competition. Of course, co-creation involves not only products, as people acknowledge and harness each other's strengths, differences and sensitivities. This is the kind of liberating culture that Kitano Seiki aims to create. Employees take pride in the efforts of predecessors who have tackled and overcome difficult challenges and then work together to create an even greater history to be passed down to future generations." All of Kitano Seiki's employees have read the above motto, which is recorded in a small pamphlet.

Every secret passed down

When asked, "How can a small-scale backstreet factory have the highly-advanced technologies and technical development prowess needed to create world-leading testing equipment?" President Masahiro Kitano responded, "Our culture is formed by a collection of people who want to create advanced equipment that no other person can." As the leader of the company, Kitano also explained, "One of my most important roles is to help us maintain and develop a great sense of pride in the company, based on the fact that we can create things that no one else in the world can." He also noted, "Some employees attempt to develop wildly experimental equipment that is seemingly impossible. I embrace this atmosphere wherever possible because it can lead to new ideas and product development."

Kitano Seiki's factory is located underground directly below its head office. It is not uncommon for the company to receive orders from universities or research institutions requiring "delivery by tomorrow," which on occasion requires working through the night, and for this reason the factory was moved underground to avoid disturbing the surrounding community with loud noises. The factory displays written slogans such as "Let's be the best partner to researchers" and "Pass down every secret." These slogans were all created by employees after they took part in group training camps away from the company. At times, employees and researchers gather together to enjoy camping or a barbecue. Kitano Seiki's true strength can be found in this down-to-earth, family-like atmosphere.

One example where Kitano Seiki has achieved great success is testing equipment for linear motors. Linear motors use the repulsive force of magnets to make a vehicle float. Powerful magnetic forces are needed to float an entire train car. Extremely low temperature equipment close to absolute zero is what makes this possible. Kitano Seiki's testing equipment is used in testing for forming this extremely low temperature.

This testing technology, while not used for the linear unit, is highly acclaimed among stakeholders as revolutionary and efforts are now underway to commercialize it as a new propulsion system for ships. This brand-new technology was independently developed by Kitano Seiki and is patented by the company.

Additionally, Kitano Seiki developed and supplied a compact electron microscope for research purposes to the Okinawa Institute of Science and Technology Graduate University. The single greatest trait of this electron microscope is that it is just one-third the size of conventional ones. Kitano Seiki developed this compact version so that it could be used in the small research labs of universities. Although it is somewhat lacking in capabilities compared to larger electron microscopes, it does provide sufficient capabilities for just about every advanced technology. Moreover, the price is much lower, to an extent where a research lab can afford it. In 2009, Kitano Seiki delivered an organic EL development system to a national research institute in Australia. This is a highly versatile development system and it has been delivered to many research institutions, helping to underpin Kitano Seiki.

Shigeo Kitano, father of the current president and founder of the company, once worked for an army research institute, but he was originally with a preparatory practice unit and at the end of World War II he was assigned to a special attack unit. After returning to civilian life, he established a metal machining company in what is today Ota Ward. Mass-produced products undermined profitability and made it impossible to increase profits, so he decided to focus on order-made production with higher profit margins. His son and second president, Masahiro, further evolved this approach and greatly transformed the company into one focused on research equipment needed by scientific researchers and sophisticated highly-advanced technologies like today. In the future, the company aims to become a development-oriented company focused primarily on design and development. With experience studying abroad, Masahiro held the ambitious dream of "becoming a company that could be a world leader even if it were small in size." He changed the company's website and product pamphlets by adding English next to the Japanese text. Some younger employees began to study English, too. Kitano Seiki is now working hard "to become a company needed not only by researchers in Japan but also those from around the world who are aiming to win a Nobel Prize."

Humble beginnings – Founded by a husband and wife in a studio apartment

RF Co., Ltd. began as RF System Research Lab, which was established by President Jiro Maruyama and his wife Yuriko in 1992 in a leased studio apartment in Nagano City. Since then, the company has created a number of new products, with a focus on microwaves, that have turned the conventional wisdom of the industry on its head. Today, RF's wireless intraoral camera for dentistry occupies a dominant share of the world market, especially in the United States where it enjoys a dominant market share. The company continues to grow exponentially every year as now it is a medium-sized enterprise that employs a workforce of 230 and has paid-in capital of approximately 1.7 billion yen. At present, it is developing a capsule endoscopy that is a revolutionary medical device and could transform colon and colorectal cancer testing if successful.

Maruyama once worked as an engineer for a major manufacturing company, but later decided to become an independent technical consultant. He met his wife Yuriko around this time and while the two got engaged, Yuriko's father greatly opposed the marriage and blocked Maruyama's way at the entrance with a stick in his hand when he tried to visit the family. Eventually they would get married. After marrying Yuriko, Maruyama established the venture company RF System Research Lab. In contrast to his grand dreams for growth of the business, in the beginning, the head office with both business and manufacturing capabilities all began in a small studio apartment in Nagano City.

Today, Japan continues to be in the middle of the third venture boom and venture business owners have seen their social status rise. In most cases, venture entrepreneurs still go to their family members, such as siblings or parents, to be their guarantors when borrowing start-up funds and working capital for their businesses. However, it is also not uncommon to see venture business owners going bankrupt or fall into huge debt when their business fails, resulting in not only their own but also their families' assets being seized.

As such, when Maruyama intended to start his own venture company he experienced the most resistance from his family. His wife's relatives presented a particularly intimidating obstacle. Luckily, he was able to have his wife on his side for starting the business.

The first-ever product made by the couple's small company was a compact CCD camera. At the time, Maruyama had predicted room for growth in the CCD field. This product was both cheaper and offered more functions than conventional CCD cameras. In addition, the product incorporated many breakthrough technologies for the CCD and camera sectors up until then. All of the above contributed to its unprecedented popularity, even though it was created by a small company run by just two people. This marked a successful beginning for the business. The next big product they shifted their attention to was wireless technology. At the time, the sending and receiving of images using wireless technology was already available in television cameras. The technology was, however, very expensive and limited to major national television stations such as NHK and was unattainable by small cable television stations. In light of this, Maruyama and his wife were consigned to create a microwave transmission device, which they had delivered to match a similar device made by major manufacturers but at 130,000 yen, which was less than one-tenth the price. Nevertheless, they were still able to make a decent profit from it.

How did RF obtain a dominant share in the United States market?

At some point, an article about a new use for cordless CCD cameras was published in the newspaper. Someone had attached one to a model train, providing aficionados with the feeling of being a passenger on their very own model railroad. After he found out about this, Maruyama created a model train car attached with a CCD camera thinking that it might sell relatively well. Looking back, Maruyama says that never in his wildest dreams would he have thought that such a product would become the driving force behind growing RF into a medium-sized enterprise with a workforce of over 200 employees.

In 1996, Michael Yoshida, a highly-experienced dentist in the United States, paid a visit to Maruyama at the company's head office in Nagano City. He began by very somberly asking Maruyama whether he could create an intraoral camera for dentistry by applying the same CCD camera used for model trains. Yoshida was in Japan for a relative's memorial service and he had traveled all the way to Nagano just to ask Maruyama this question. When first asked, Maruyama did not even know what was meant by an "intraoral camera."

Yoshida explained that intraoral cameras were widely used by dentists in the United States, but were expensive and had a very long cable attached, so dentists had to rest this cable over their shoulders in order to display the patient's mouth on a television screen, resulting in a good deal of physical exertion. Yoshida desperately asked Maruyama to develop a wireless version because it could free dentists from this painful experience.

Although he did not even know that such a medical device existed in the world of dentistry, Maruyama was convinced that RF's technologies and know-how could be used to create one, so he immediately set out to do so. The devices RF had created up to that point in time were completely unrelated to medical devices. First, since it would be used inside people's mouths, RF had to figure out any sanitary issues a camera may pose. There was also a need to solve the issue of glass lenses fogging up in people's mouths, blocking the light and preventing a clear image from being taken. The issue of a fogged-up lens was solved by opening a hole in the lens cover, but the bigger issue was the need to stream video taken inside the mouth to a television monitor clearly. RF already had the technology and know-how to get this footage to the television monitor, but now it had to imbed all of these functions inside the device and make it compact enough so it could be easily used inside someone's mouth.

The thought, "I've really got myself into a pickle," crossed his mind several times, but Maruyama and RF's engineers tested it out on themselves and 18 months later, in the autumn of 1997, they had completed their very first intraoral camera. Later, the camera was tested countless times on every single employee and then the product was delivered to Yoshida the next spring. Maruyama knew that he and his colleagues had done a great job after receiving a telephone call from Yoshida who exclaimed, "Amazing! Very good!"

However, irrespective of how good the product was, just because Yoshida, who brought the idea to RF, was happy with it, did not mean that the product would result in a lot of business.

The problem was how to roll out the product in the United States. Such a small venture firm like RF had close to no employees who were proficient in English, including Maruyama himself. RF took out an ad in the local newspaper looking for people with the necessary linguistic skills. The company was able to secure the right people, given the rise in interest in foreign languages after Nagano was selected to host the Winter Olympics in 1998. Yet, no matter how proficient these human resources were, actually deploying the business targeting dentists in the United States, which is 25 times larger than Japan, proved to be elusive. Most Japanese companies have sales offices in countries around the world and request sales be performed by major Japanese trading companies, which had much better access to information. Maruyama elected against this route and embarked on creating sales channels himself. However, no matter the sales strategy, it was difficult to identify a way of deploying the business in the United States. Just at this time, Maruyama was flipping through the pages of a dentistry magazine brought back by an employee doing market research in the United States when he came up with the idea of placing an ad in the magazine.

Soon thereafter, RF placed a large color ad in the magazine for dentists in Los Angeles. A similar ad was placed inside a specialized magazine for dentists with a publication run of 150,000 copies covering the entire United States. Several days later, a letter arrived asking to see the actual product. Maruyama's decision had paid off.

After the ads were placed, letters and telephone inquiries began pouring in. Some dentists sent cash in the mail, but the majority said they wanted to see the real thing and purchase one if possible. One failure of RF's sales strategy was that the real thing could not be shown to dentists in the United States, but to make up for this, RF decided to send out a catalogue. While taking orders, RF also embarked on a comprehensive direct mail strategy by compiling a list of members of the American Dental Association. RF's ability to capture a dominant share of the United States market began initially from this direct mail strategy.

Undaunted by harassment in the Japanese market

RF's business in the United States steadily grew using this format. On the other hand, RF announced the release of a cordless intraoral camera for the Japan market in September 1997. At the time, dentists in Japan were using intraoral cameras imported from the United States, but RF's product was one-fifth the cost, plus it did not have a cord and was easy to use. A major Japanese manufacturer approached RF about an OEM production opportunity. The extraordinary condition required an order for 7,000 to 8,000 units at around 700,000 yen per unit. Maruyama turned down this offer because RF could sell the exact same product directly for around 220,000 yen. The medical device industry is made up of various associations and RF was invited to become affiliated with business circles, but also turned these down. Unfortunately, RF and its decision to go it alone was met with harassment by others in the industry.

In conjunction with meetings and academic conferences of the Japan Dental Association, medical device companies often hold exhibitions showcasing their products. However, RF never received notice of these exhibitions and it was not allocated space for its own exhibitions. The next form of harassment was the refusal of RF's ads. RF had placed one page ads every month in a specialized dentistry magazine, but this magazine contacted RF saying it could no longer accept the ad. Other magazines, too, followed suit and refused to place RF's ads. At first, RF was puzzled as to why its ads were declined, but the company soon found out that the largest sponsors of these magazines were dental device manufacturers. It was obvious these companies pressured the magazines to stop accepting ads from RF.

Around this time, when RF could no longer place its ads, the sales persons of other companies intentionally started a rumor that RF's finances were deteriorating to the point it could no longer afford to place ads. Among the dentists who believed in RF's products, some began believing that RF had exited the business. RF began receiving countless prank telephone calls saying "I heard you went bankrupt" and "Your company is about to go under and your checks are bouncing." RF never used checks before, so it was impossible for its checks to be rejected. Current Executive Vice President Naomi Karasawa joined the company soon after its incorporation and she was seen as a Company Madonna of sorts due to her cheerful disposition and talent. Yet around this time, she desperately had to hold back tears when answering these calls. After hanging up, she would head out to the end of the hallway and openly cry out loud.

In response to this harassment, RF appealed to dentists about the need for intraoral cameras using direct mail. Furthermore, RF placed protest advertisements for three consecutive months in eight prominent weekly magazines that explained that there were dentists who could treat patients using video images taken from inside the mouth. After that, homemakers with children began calling and writing to dentists who were using intraoral cameras. Maruyama came up with the idea of RF providing intraoral cameras to kindergartens and elementary schools nationwide in conjunction with cavity prevention week. Then, it opened company stores in Tokyo, Yokohama, Nagoya and other major cities near railway stations to sell directly to dentists across Japan. Huge billboards displaying RF in vivid deep red were placed on these buildings in locations with the most light. At this point, RF's strategy was the clear winner, no matter how you looked at it. The dental device manufacturers who had applied the pressure were left with egg on their faces.

Today, RF is pouring all its energy into endoscopes that you swallow. Stomach endoscope cameras are now easier to use thanks to ongoing improvements. However, the experience is still not pleasant. The unpleasantness rises to a whole other level for colon and colorectal endoscopes which have to be fed through the anus. There are many people who avoid these exams entirely because the endoscope is fed through the anus, even though they may feel the need to have colon and colorectal cancer exams. RF's endoscopes are used for colon and colorectal exams, but instead of being fed through the large intestine and colon from the anus like conventional endoscopes, they are capsule shaped with a length of 23 millimeters and a diameter of 9 millimeters. This is roughly the same or slightly larger than the capsule medication prescribed at hospitals. Just like pharmaceuticals, these endoscopes are swallowed.

The capsule uses magnets to spin around while inside the large intestine and colon and take ultra-close-up photographs of the entire digestive tract spanning six to eight meters.

Images are recorded as one long, continuous strip and show the round pipe-shaped digestive tract as if it was cut open by scissors, so it is possible to measure the dimensions and areas of diseased parts together with the passing of time. Images can also be enlarged under high magnification or played together like a video to check the small movements of the digestive cells. The lens faces laterally so the entirety of the walls can be photographed without omission. The cameras are powered wirelessly, so there is no need to embed a battery in them. The capsule comes out in a bowel movement once its job is over, so it can be flushed down the toilet and discarded.

Major Japanese endoscope companies and overseas companies are working on the development of the same type of endoscopes, but Maruyama says with great confidence, "RF is overwhelmingly superior in almost every way." The name of this capsule is Sayaka. Most of RF's products have a female name. One third of RF's managers, general managers and senior management are women. This is the result of adopting a performance-based system.

RF is also a company with a "very female-friendly work environment," says Karasawa.

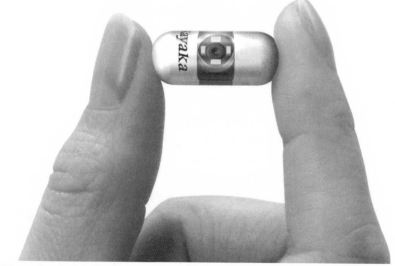

RF capsule endoscope, Sayaka

Fixing the issue of blurry images

The world of nano-technology involves creating ultra-precise products on the order of one millionth of a millimeter and one billionth of a gram. This is an industry that will shape the 21st century and many people believe that Japan has the world's leading nano-technologies. ELIONIX INC. (Hachioji City, Tokyo) has produced a number of high-tech devices utilizing nano-technologies and know-how, including electron beam lithography systems, electron beam 3D roughness analysis equipment and electron beam machining systems. It is a small company with a workforce of 93 employees and sales of over 2.6 billion yen, but nearly all of the equipment and systems it produces are one of a kind and can only be made by Elionix. Most of its products are for research use or semi-finished production, requiring confidentiality agreements with customers. Certain details are unavailable due to confidentiality agreements and patents, but Elionix has succeeded in a myriad of highly-advanced industries, including camera lenses without diffuse reflection and solutions that speed up optical communication, among others. Elionix is recognized as a niche firm and a global leader by the Ministry of Economy, Trade and Industry.

Elionix's very first product after its founding was a device for ultra-fine machining that emitted an electron beam using special materials. This device formed a major foundation for the company and it remains one of its mainstay products. The initial device was able to machine from 50 nanometers to 100 nanometers. The next-generation model improved performance up to less than 10 nanometers. The latest device in the same series is able to machine up to less than 4 nanometers and the machining speed initially took close to ten days to create one pattern, but this has been shortened to between one and two hours. Although it varies depending on the material being machined and the precision required, compared to the initial device, the latest version offers 50 to 100 times greater performance.

Ultra-fine machining is used in advanced industries such as mobile phones, smartphones, cameras and semiconductors, to name a few, but the most prominent is cameras. In the past, ordinary people taking photographs most often made the mistake of moving their hands when pressing the shutter, resulting in a blurry and unfocused image. However, almost no cameras these days take blurry images, even if the photographer moves their hand slightly. Now people can take beautiful photographs without having to worry about the focus. The secret behind this improved camera performance can be found in Elionix's devices.

The most important way to prevent blurry images taken on a camera is first and foremost to improve lens performance. Conventional optics-based devices were unable to carry out ultra-fine machining of the lens on the tens-of-thousandths-of-a-millimeter level. However, electron beams are able to machine on a nano level. This has improved lens performance beyond people's wildest imaginations. This also led to a significant size reduction in camera lenses. This technology is also applied to cameras used on mobile phones. That is, compact cameras and smartphone cameras that can be held in one hand can now easily take beautiful photographs. Since a camera is an advanced precision device, it is not made up of Elionix's technologies exclusively, but without a doubt the company has greatly contributed to the development of cameras today.

In the space of just three decades, mobile phones have changed from analog to digital and now feature a weight and battery life that are nothing like the first models. Additionally, mobile phones are no longer just a phone; rather they have been transformed into an all-in-one information device that can play music, shoot videos and play video games. Such advancements required ultra-compact devices and greatly improved performance and Elionix's ultra-fine machining devices have been widely used in research and development in these fields. These devices have contributed to improved performance in a myriad of fields, including semiconductors and automobiles, and in terms of future fields, they are being used for research and to create products in healthcare, such as injection needles made of ultra-fine tubes that you don't even feel when they pierce your skin.

Technologies that no other company can come close to replicating

Elionix's Surface Roughness Analysis 3D Scanning Electron Microscope analyzes substances and materials used mainly at analysis centers and research labs. It can measure and observe at a maximum magnification of one million times. This by itself suggests it is the same as a conventional electron beam microscope, but as the name indicates, Elionix's product analyzes the surface of specimens three dimensionally.

An electron beam microscope, too, can certainly view substances at several tens of thousands of times magnification. However, even if the structure of a substance or its accuracy can be observed, two dimensional images cannot be used to analyze the depth or height of holes or protrusions on its surface. Elionix's device not only offers several tens of thousands of times magnification, it can measure the surface of substances three dimensionally, so the size of uneven texture and even the depth of holes can be analyzed as they are displayed clearly on the device's attached LCD screen.

This enables measurement in high resolution on a nano level and viewing images from a bird's-eye view. New materials for advanced technologies using nano-technology resulted in the issue whereby even though the constituent parts are analyzed and found to be unproblematic, defects in performance and quality are found. However, using Elionix's device, the cause can be clearly identified and analysis can be performed, from the unevenness of highly-advanced materials and products to problematic areas on the surface, which until now was seen as impossible. Many prefectural technology centers in Japan naturally want to purchase this device for the new product development and product improvements of local SMEs and medium-sized enterprises.

In terms of its load-controlled indentation tester, Elionix has no rival in Japan and only a handful of companies in the world can compete with it. The indentations of diamonds, considered the hardest substance on earth, can be embedded into material using microscopic loads and, by measuring the microscopic changes of indentations, the hardness of the surface is measured. This makes it possible to inspect the hardness of a surface, modulus of elasticity and Young's modulus on a nano level.

It may be difficult to understand the benefits offered by analyzing the surface of material in an ultra-fine manner. This device is most often used for films, ceramics, metal materials and carbon fiber used in large quantities in next-generation automotive chassis. It can test the hardness of a thin film surface on electronic parts, such as large-scale integration, thin films of semiconductor substrates that are becoming denser and polymeric materials, which are considered to be difficult to measure by conventional means.

This device will be used to advance the development of excellent nano-scale products that are essential for the leading industries of the 21st century by enabling the creation of new materials or the modification of materials that were previously impossible. Electron beam nano welding devices that are used for the formation of metallic nano particles and that can weld on the microscopic and nano level have enabled welding in areas that humans previously could not control. Electron beam disc mastering devices are essential to the manufacture of beyond-next-generation magnetic disks that far exceed the capabilities of next-generation magnetic disks. Some of Elionix's products are being used not only in next-generation research, but also beyond-next-generation research, looking ahead to 10 and 20 years into the future. Elionix's customers include advanced-research organizations such as the Japan Aerospace Exploration Agency (JAXA), the High Energy Accelerator Research

Organization and the International Superconductivity Technology Center, as well as renowned national and private universities, such as the University of Tokyo, Kyoto University, Tokyo Institute of Technology, Keio University and Tokyo University of Science. Elionix also works with major corporations such as Canon, Sony and Toshiba and even with Harvard University and the Massachusetts Institute of Technology (MIT) in the United States. This speaks volumes about the advanced level of Elionix's technological prowess. Elionix's strengths include not only its world-leading testers and machining devices for ultra-fine machining on a nanometer level, but also the fact that its markets themselves are extremely niche.

Elionix's only rivals are a company in Japan, a company in the United Kingdom and a company in Germany. Elionix maintains a dominant 80% share of the Japan market and a 50% share of the international market for electron beam lithography systems. For this reason, customers rarely demand lower prices and there are virtually no cases where Elionix is forced to compete with rival companies over the price of the products it delivers. Elionix's devices are created with highly-advanced, cutting-edge technologies that it would be very difficult for any other company to replicate and have been a great success in the company's business strategy of focusing on niche markets.

Committed to manufacturing in Japan and not exporting to China or South Korea

Let's take a closer look at Elionix's production methods. Product planning and design are carried out in-house, but everything from device components to assembly and wiring are all outsourced. Within the manufacturing process, Elionix is responsible only for the assembly of important parts, calibration, inspection and delivery. Many companies with advanced technologies prefer to develop not only parts, but also the machinery that makes these parts, internally.

Elionix conversely uses an extensive outside network. One reason is the location of Elionix in Tokyo. There are a large number of SMEs in the Tama region of Tokyo that can create advanced parts and materials for electronics and precision devices. The fact that Elionix is located in an area with a supply of advanced parts and materials is one of the reasons why it is a world-leading company.

Elionix is not considering moving its manufacturing processes offshore. This is because it is difficult for the company to procure the necessary advanced parts and materials outside of Japan and the risk of counterfeit products that arises with switching production to another country. In order to avoid the risk of counterfeit products being made locally if it expanded into China or other emerging countries, Elionix carefully ensures that it only exports products with highly-advanced technologies that cannot be counterfeited to China and South Korea.

As evidenced by their use in research institutes, universities and advanced technology industries, most of Elionix's products are used in fields involving highly-advanced technologies, so Elionix's approach to sales and marketing differs rather markedly from ordinary companies. Elionix's chairman, president and other senior management utilize their personal networks developed over countless years to visit university professors, national and local research institutions and the executives of private sector research labs in an effort to better understand the needs of customers. Salespersons travel with engineers to listen directly to customers about their needs and then use this information in product development and sales. The greatest advantages for Elionix's sales are the company's strong personal networks and its approach of conducting "proposal-based sales."

Proposal-based sales requires talented people. "Human resource development is our greatest investment," believes Chairman Seigo Honme. Elionix has emphasized human resources development and investing in its human capital. In principle, the company does not make mid-career hires and instead focuses on university graduates and graduates of vocational high schools. In order to develop engineers, Elionix partners veteran employees engaged in device development with young engineers in their second or third year at the company as part of its mechanism to develop new products requiring advanced technologies or large devices. It has been about ten years since Elionix adopted this approach to developing young engineers. This has greatly contributed to the development of the company's engineers and produced engineers who play a central role in successful development.

Just as how veteran employees have a hard time explaining to their family what exactly they do at work, although Elionix has become a well-known company in the nano-tech world, it remains virtually unknown by the rest of society. Besides that, most members of the general public would still probably not understand the type of work Elionix does even if you were to explain it to them. Nevertheless, Elionix's retention rate is extremely high, as President Tetsuyuki Okabayashi says, "Although some employees have quit due to unavoidable reasons, such as family, there are virtually no employees who quit for other reasons." This is largely due to the fact that employees are given the chance to manage major projects from a young age and they have a sense of pride in working for one of the few world-leading companies in the area of highly-advanced technologies.

Successful transition of management policy

Elionix was founded by seven people who had worked with JEOL, a major manufacturer of electron devices. Three of them had a background in electronics and electron beams, two in machinery and two in physics. The goal of the company initially was to develop devices that applied each of their specializations, which were electronics, ion beams and x-rays. The name of the company originates from the first letter or first few letters of each of these specializations. At first, Elionix did outsourcing work for major corporations and worked on research devices for Nippon Telegraph and Telephone Public Corporation's (currently NTT) research lab. In the past, this research lab was one of the world's foremost information communication research institutions with technical prowess and a workforce so talented that it could have produced Nobel Prize winners. The fact that Elionix did business with such a prestigious organization demonstrates that the company had a truly advanced level of technical prowess from the very beginning.

Although it was a semiconductor and equipment-related company, the collapse of Japan's asset bubble is what spurred Elionix's transformation into its current form as a nano-tech equipment manufacturer. The collapse of Japan's asset bubble caused orders to drop in half, making entry into new fields an urgent task. Because it saw limitations in the future of semiconductors and determined that it was fully possible for it to enter the nano-tech field thanks to its accumulated technologies, Elionix completely shifted its management strategy. The perfect timing of this decision is what propelled Elionix to become a global manufacturer of nano-tech lithography and analysis equipment.

Technologies refined at the nano level

A major strength of Japan is the fact that it is home to many small-scale, backstreet workshops that are not only world leaders in nano-tech, but also lead the world in unique, proprietary technologies. Based in the outskirts of Sendai City in Miyagi Prefecture, TDC Corporation is a prominent example of an SME with highly-advanced technologies.

TDC machines and polishes surfaces with ultra-precision, meaning that it uses technologies to polish materials until they are like the surface of a mirror. A unique aspect about the company's operations is that it polishes the surface of materials on a nano level. TDC possesses some of the world's foremost ultra-precise surface-machining technologies that are used on the nano level for materials in various fields, from Japan's prominent high-tech industries, such as cutting-edge hybrid vehicles, electronics, electronic components, industrial tools, to fields that will pave the way for the future of Japan's economy, including medical devices and space industries.

Moreover, TDC doesn't just polish materials that are easy to polish, such as a mirror made from glass, but polishes nearly every industrial material, from well-known metals, such as stainless steel, nickel and copper, to rare metals like molybdenum and tungsten, as well as ceramics, such as alumina, titania and yttrium, and everyday materials such as acrylic and polycarbonate. The precision of polishing depends on the materials, but in most cases TDC is able to finish on the nano level. Also, it can polish to achieve flatness at a scale of 30 nanometers. TDC can machine at around 100 nanometers for dimensions, parallelness, straightness and angles. This means TDC is able to machine the volume and weight of cubic shapes at tolerances of 0.01 grams. TDC is believed to be the only company in Japan capable of machining and polishing with this level of accuracy.

TDC's polishing machines consist of a surface plate that materials are placed on top of, a drive mechanism that moves the surface plate, a device that moves packing materials for polishing and a device that supplies slurry for polishing. To begin, raw polishing is performed with extremely fine diamond grains on the six micron level (0.006 millimeters) and once a certain size of mirror surface is created from this process, next, half of the diamond grains are used to further polish. Depending on the materials, this is also when solvent is added to form an oil membrane on the three-micron level. Finishing uses one-micrometer grains to polish the surface all the way to the nano level. This machining process also involves grinding the materials extremely finely. The grinding amount when the material is rotated once and the grinding amount per minute are adjusted with extreme precision.

Polishing and ultra-fine grinding rely heavily on the manual labor of employees and are performed jointly between machines and people. Products made in this manner "are used across various fields, so much so you could never guess which one they are destined for," explained President Ryoya Akabane, but typically products are bound for semiconductor manufacturing equipment, LCD-related equipment, medical devices, optical equipment, automobiles, printing machines, as well as research institutions and university research labs. TDC supplies more than 3,000 companies in Japan and outside of Japan. Its technologies were also used in the development of hybrid vehicles, a field where Japan excels. Although part of TDC's factory was damaged during the earthquake that struck the Tohoku region of Japan in 2011, it escaped any damage from the tsunami and its production was barely affected. Nevertheless, most of the company's customers were anxious to find out if the company's production was affected by the disaster, because it is indispensable to many businesses and industries.

TDC makes most of the machinery it uses

In addition to the nano-technologies that are the company's pride and joy, TDC also believes in the importance of providing highly detailed services that make it possible to accommodate customer requests in a short period of time. It has also established a structure that enables it to fulfill orders that for whatever reason need to be delivered the next day. While accepting mass-produced items on the one hand, TDC is also able to handle single unit orders. One reason, says President Akabane, is because "SMEs cannot survive unless they can fulfil the requests of every single customer." At the same time, it is also because TDC's production system and production facilities can accommodate all orders, from a single unit to mass production. TDC employs a team of 60. Its production facilities include 85 one-sided lapping machines, 15 two-sided lapping machines, 24 grinding machines, as well as machining tools such as machining centers, milling machines, lathes and electrical discharge machines, which outnumber its employees on the production floor by more than two to one. That is why TDC can say "We'll accept any order." If it did not have the necessary system in place, it could not make such a statement in good faith. TDC's management policy also reveals many lessons about how to survive and thrive as an SME.

While TDC orders some of its machinery from machine tool manufacturers, most of the machinery used by TDC was made by TDC. One of the main reasons for this is because there are few manufacturers who can create this machinery given the highly-advanced technologies involved. More so, this is to prevent the leakage of technical information by using its own production facilities and due to the fact that TDC can create machines that are extremely easy to use. The loss of technological information by major Japanese manufacturers during offshoring has become a serious issue as of late. This issue is far more serious for SMEs, not only because they face the threat of loss of information, but also because major corporations could create virtually the same product by carefully finding a way around their patents and then mass-produce them. This would result in the eventual bankruptcy or reduced operations of the SME. For this reason, TDC prohibits all access to its factory by non-employees. TDC is able to safeguard its proprietary technologies by making its own production equipment and keeping its production floor isolated from outsiders.

Local human resources play key roles

TDC was established in 1953 as Tohoku Die Cast Co. Ltd. The current incarnation of TDC was born in 1989. As its name indicated, back when TDC was known as "Tohoku Die Cast," it was a manufacturer of die casts used in mass-produced electrical and electronic parts. However, in the 1980s, Japan's electrical and electronic parts industry began to rapidly move production offshore. TDC's finances deteriorated rapidly because it was exposed to competition with overseas production and the corresponding labor costs, which were far lower than those of Japan. As a means of survival, TDC decided to begin offering ceramic polishing, using its polishing and grinding technologies for die cast parts. During the process of developing proprietary ceramic polishing technologies, in 1998 it established ultra-fine polishing technologies that were as yet unheard of. Soon this business grew into its own and orders began to come in for polishing on the 50-nanometer level. According to President Akabane, the company focused earnestly on advancing its proprietary technologies without considering the relationship with nano-technologies, so "At the time, I didn't even know what the word 'nano' meant, let alone the term 'nano-technology.'"

Around this time, there was a rapidly growing number of SMEs driven to the point of bankruptcy because production bases were offshored by parent companies. TDC decided that the only way it could survive in Japan was "nano-technology," and by 1999 it had improved its technical prowess to the point that it could produce machined products on the 10-nanometer level. Tohoku University is one of Japan's foremost universities with advanced research functions where each year several of its professors are among the candidates for a Nobel Prize. Among this research, the university is known for its impressive track record in material engineering, including metallurgical engineering. An emeritus professor with Tohoku University specializing in material engineering had taught that polishing metals at 10 nanometers or below was impossible. They didn't believe it when TDC said they had the technologies to do this, but were extremely surprised when they saw for themselves that it was actually possible.

Since then, this emeritus professor has introduced TDC to Tohoku University students and provided technical advice to the company and TDC remains thankful to this individual even today as their efforts helped in many ways to improve TDC's technologies to this point. TDC has been able to rapidly improve its technologies thanks in part to this type of support from researchers.

Meanwhile, underpinned by the Act on Supporting Business Innovation of Small and Medium Enterprises, in 2000 TDC received approval from Miyagi Prefecture for its management reform plan and in 2001 TDC received a 77 New Business Grant from the 77 Business Support Foundation established by 77 Bank, Tohoku's largest financial institution. Later, in 2004, TDC received a grant to defray the costs of new growth industries after its plan to enter a new growth industry was approved by Miyagi Prefectural Government. Additionally, TDC's research into large-surface, ultra-precise machining method was adopted for the commercialization R&D program (grant) of the fiscal 2007 SME/Venture support project. TDC is a classic example of an SME improving its technologies by skillfully utilizing various grants from the national government and local financial institution.

TDC is a company on par with the world's foremost companies in highly-advanced technologies and yet a majority of its workforce graduated from local high schools. TDC possesses truly exceptional measurement equipment that even national research institutes rarely have access to. Because of its high price and ultra-precision, TDC's measurement equipment cannot be used by other companies except when they employ specialists. At TDC, however, every employee is able to use this measurement equipment freely. This makes it possible for them to measure whether the product they made meets the precision requirements of the customer, which, in itself is highly beneficial, but what is more, it means that TDC can also measure the level of its production capability, at the same time as it manufactures products.

Now that they can freely measure accuracy, employees have been able to expand their originality and to further whet their appetite for innovation and ingenuity. This goes beyond just measuring the level of precision. TDC's employees are able to consider and put into practice ways to increase this precision further and ways to ensure products are finished quicker. In the past, very few TDC employees worked on product creation according to their own unique approaches, but as a result of fostering an environment where employees can freely measure results and work hard, the company's production efficiency has increased.

Being able to reward the originality and ingenuity of every individual

TDC established the TDC Award to commend employees who successfully helped the company to create excellent products or improve quality. This award system helped to complete a breakthrough technology.

One day, a company placed an order with TDC for the ultra-precise machining of a part from one of its strategic products. After a TDC competitor worked on several prototypes but couldn't produce satisfactory results, the company came to TDC expecting that it could complete the part. The competitor had said the request was impossible. While the angle had to be around 20 nanometers, plus or minus three arc seconds, the angled surface had to be machined extremely precisely at one nanometer or less and the width of the ridgeline where the angle joined had to be kept at tolerances of 150 nanometers or less.

Even for TDC and its advanced technologies, a product requiring such ultra-fine precision was impossible using conventional approaches. However, in order to achieve the ultra-precise angles, surface and dimensions, a highly-skilled TDC employee came up with a completely new jig for machining, which made it possible to fulfill the customer's precision requirements. This machine tool was extremely creative and completely went against conventional wisdom. Moreover, the structure of this jig could be applied to other machined products, so since then, this jig, named after the employee who created it, has been used for many years now with great success, earning its inventor an award for developing it. This award is only given out once every several years, but every few years between 7 and 8 employees are presented with the TDC Award. This award system has been in place for more than a decade, with more than 100 employees being selected for the honor. This accumulation of technology has become a major asset for TDC.

Normally the award is accompanied with a cash prize of 10,000 yen, which can increase all the way up to 100,000 yen. Akabane encourages every employee to try to win an award by saying, "Everyone who pushes themselves has a chance of winning." The cash prize is one appeal of the award, but more important is motivating employees, as employee awareness improves a great deal if their achievements are recognized. Employees who graduated from a local high school have received an award. There are also mid-career hires who have been chosen to receive an award. President Akabane explained his management philosophy as, "We're a small company, so I make it a point to treat everyone well and reward the originality and ingenuity of every employee." Thus, TDC is able to cultivate knowledge and ingenuity thanks to its efforts to motivate its people.

TDC often concludes a confidentiality agreement when signing a contract with customers. Safeguarding the company's technologies is not the only goal behind this. A confidentiality agreement also ensures that the customer's secrets are protected as well. TDC's products are frequently used in highly-advanced technologies, so customers could suffer immeasurable losses if these technologies were divulged. There are even cases where the very act of engaging in joint research with TDC is a secret. This is because for competitors, simply knowing that joint research is taking place with TDC will infringe upon important secrets. TDC was selected as a top global niche company by the Ministry of Economy, Trade and Industry, which stands as proof of its status as an excellent SME. TDC's ultra-precise, nano-scale polishing technologies were used on parts of the Hayabusa2 asteroid exploration mission. TDC has set itself the ambitious goal of becoming a global company with a unique status earned by developing original technologies.

Chapter 4

Controlling Niche Markets Inaccessible to Big Firms

Six Companies – "No Need for an Administrative Department"

The fields where SMEs specialize are niche markets that big companies cannot get into. But the case is often that many of these business categories were not always in existence. In fact, most of them were created by the SMEs themselves. Surviving in a niche market is no picnic for an SME. It requires them to sweat and exert themselves to create that new market. The products invented in the niche markets Japanese SMEs have built up are among the best in the world and in many cases their absence could affect international economic activity.

How does the elevator stop on a dime?

Metrol Co., Ltd., based in Tachikawa, Tokyo, makes mechanical switches for setting precise locations. These switches accurately measure and control positions for the movements of machine tools, semiconductor manufacturing equipment and other machinery. At first glance, it may seem that these components have little impact on our lives, but it is thanks to Metrol's switches that elevators can stop on a dime without even being a millimeter off. The company's switches have been utilized recently for medical instruments used in neurosurgery, helping to save the lives of numerous patients suffering from intractable diseases. Metrol is nearly the only company in the world in this field, with a global market share of 70%. The secret behind Metrol's ability to retain a top share of the global market, despite being an SME with a workforce of just over 100 employees, can be found in how the company has literally bet its existence on manufacturing and craftsmanship by taking on the challenges of advanced technology and how it has a thoroughly streamlined administration where departments like human resources and accounting do not even exist.

A cutting machine would be the prototypical example of a machine tool. It is equipped with blades for cutting metal. No matter how good the machine tool is, if the blades are not mounted in a precise position, then it cannot perform well. Also, although the blades are made from a special metal that is incredibly hard, after millions or tens of millions of cutting actions, any blade is bound to crack and move out of position. If this goes unnoticed and the machinery continues to operate, it will experience a failure. It used to be that experienced employees with decades in their profession would identify misalignments and chipped blades from the subtle movements and changes in the sounds produced by the machines. Using their experience and intuition, they would make adjustments.

But with positioning switches developed by Metrol, a manufacturer can automatically stop machines when chipped blades will result in defective products. They can even bring machinery to a halt immediately before a misalignment results in a non-conformity. This eliminates the need for experienced employees to constantly check the machines and allows for a production line to be fully automated. And when that line operates 24 hours a day, it yields a productivity gain. Even after executing over 3 million actions, Metrol's switches will initiate a stop when a misalignment of only 0.0005 to 0.0010 mm occurs. They also have a similar sensitivity when detecting chipped blades. Switch prices vary depending on the type, but they can range from a few thousand yen to more than 100,000 yen. There are two types of positioning switches: those that employ mechanical functions like Metrol's and others that use light and magnetic waves.

There was a time when optical and magnetic switches were in heavy use and were mostly manufactured by big electronics makers. These switches would amplify light or magnetism to control machinery, but their undisputed shortcoming was thermal vulnerability. Machine tools emit magnetic waves as well as high levels of heat. Moreover, some machines disperse bits of cut metal or leak oil, which can have an adverse effect on switch performance, reducing accuracy. On the other hand, Metrol's mechanical switches are thermal resistant because they do not use light or magnetic waves and remain quite accurate even under challenging conditions involving oil or flying bits of metal. Furthermore, Metrol's mechanical switches are far more affordable than optical and magnetic switches, as they carry about one-tenth of the price.

During the global financial crisis of 2007-2008, even sales at Metrol fell by more than 50%. Two years later, however, the recovery in exports, where the company makes most of its sales, brought business back up to pre-crisis levels. In the fiscal year beginning April 1, 2014, Metrol achieved even higher sales of 1.5 billion yen, demonstrating the company's strong international competitiveness. This is an example showing that even an SME, if it possesses technology that outdoes anything else in the world, can overcome an unprecedented recession and maintain a stable business.

Fierce resistance to corporate theft by a larger rival

Akira Matsuhashi, the father of current Metrol President Takuji Matsuhashi, founded the company. He was an engineer who graduated after studying at the Department of Precision Engineering, which is part of the University of Tokyo's Faculty of Engineering. He found a job at a big camera maker, where he worked on developing an endoscope and produced a practical design for a first-generation, commercially-available model. This is a time when medicine had not achieved the advances of today. Many people died of stomach cancer, not to mention gastric ulcers as well. Akira thought that being able to look inside the stomach with a camera could save many patients' lives, so he was very motivated as an engineer. However, the company's management exhibited no understanding whatsoever about endoscopes. Instead management resisted development, arguing that if anybody got hurt in an endoscope experiment it would tarnish the company's reputation. Therefore, Akira kept his endoscope research secret as he worked on developing consumer cameras for the next seven years. In the end, his perseverance was rewarded with success. The endoscope he developed was later covered by Japan's health insurance system. Later models employed fiber optics and helped make this company grow into the world's largest maker of endoscopes.

And yet, despite the great things developers did when they were first working on the structural design of an endoscope that would satisfy physicians' desire to take photographs inside the stomach, the company did not reward them, regardless of the central role this technology held within its business. In fact, the company was apparently quite indifferent to their achievements. There was a backlash against this policy and Akira decided to establish Metrol because he wanted to "make a company that rewards the engineers who sweat and work hard to make a contribution to society." The name of the company is a portmanteau of "measure" and "control."

Soon after Akira created his business, a larger company stole a critical technology developed by Metrol. It was not yet patented and the larger company would not even listen to any objections. Enraged, Akira sent a letter of protest straight to that company's leadership, informed them of the facts and succeeded in negotiating a licensing agreement. Metrol thus overcame a threat to its survival. Today, Metrol vibrantly upholds that defiant spirit of bravely standing up to those who steal its technology.

Own the order—no planned production

Metrol's production method employs the Japanese concept of *ikko nagashi*. This term, which can be translated literally as "one-piece flow," entails an individual person handling the entire process from receiving an order to production, inspection and packaging. It also means no production catering to anticipated demand. President Matsuhashi said, "The greatest saying about our company is that we do not even know what jobs we are going to do three weeks from now." Metrol keeps no inventory whatsoever and takes orders for one item at a time. The thing that does the most to make this production system possible is the company's proprietary order reception and production system. That is because it ensures there is never a surplus or shortage of parts, as the system orders parts in the quantities needed for each individual order as it comes in. According to Matsuhashi, "We always respond in real time and we are not at all considering using planned production in the future."

No matter what kinds of inquiries or orders Metrol receives from users or customers, the company can always provide an estimate and come up with a production plan detailing delivery dates and other information, all within one day. This means that in addition to being able to provide products to Japanese users in a minimum number of days, Metrol can also deliver to most regions of the world within one week.

Decisions via email strictly prohibited

Metrol never holds meetings to share information about the business. Employees instead do this via a closed blogging system for internal use only. Most of the company's important decisions are made when employees meet over coffee in the office. They are not allowed to decide matters over internal email; all decisions are made face-to-face.

There are no separate rooms or partitions between sections of the office. This makes it easy for workers to meet anyone at any time. Department section managers do not have their own rooms. Not even the president has his own office. All employees work in an open office space in a layout that is not determined by one's position.

The president performs his work in the middle of the office so that anybody can talk with him directly when they need to.

The factory operations department is located on the second floor of the plant and it uses the same open office layout. The factory and the office are connected by four flights of stairs. If somebody from the production department needs to meet with a counterpart in the office, they can simply climb one of the staircases. Conversely, if someone from the office needs to go see a person in the production department, they can walk downstairs. But the system is of no use at all if the people in it do not get along. To foster smooth communication between employees, Metrol places importance on both office communication and *nomyunication*, a Japanese portmanteau of *nomu* ("to drink") and "communication." This term refers to building camaraderie over alcoholic beverages. Members of the management team carry credit cards in the company's name which they can use for the company to pay for employee get-togethers over drinks when they are deemed necessary. Interacting at a pub or bar stimulates further communication in the workplace and invigorates the workforce.

Another source of Metrol's strength is the production system the company has established for making high-precision products. There are 7,000 parts required to make Metrol's 700 different products, but most employees go through a standardized training and practice regimen that allows them to devise tools and evenly spread out work so that they do not have to possess advanced proficiency in order to carry out their tasks.

Around 80% of the roughly 60 assembly workers are women working part-time. Most are typical housewives who live in apartments or houses near the factory. Women are a key part of Metrol's success. Their working hours are between 9:30 a.m. and 4:30 p.m. so they can also raise children. The company enrolls them in Employees' Pension Insurance, Unemployment Insurance and other programs in Japan's Social Insurance system. They also receive bonuses three times a year. The part-time female employees are considered "permanent employees with shorter working hours."

All employees get together for parties held three times a year. These events begin at 4 o'clock, before the working day is officially over, but those last 30 minutes are still paid. Generally, all employees are involved in planning the parties. They end at 5:30 p.m. and are arranged so that employees can go pick up their children at daycare and maintain a work-life balance. Part-timers are generally on one-year contracts, but these are usually renewed unless there is a good reason not to, for example if the employee is not suited to the job. Nearly 100% of them get new contracts with higher wages. "At our company, we have our female part-time employees play an important role, too." Metrol makes maximum use of these women's abilities and offering them a women-friendly workplace goes a long way toward doing so.

Metrol gets over 300 suggestions a year for improving or changing the way it works. That is more than three times the number of employees. Many of these suggestions also come from part-time workers. Making these suggestions is in line with the company's policies, which most of the employees understand. Metrol may be kind to its workers, but they are expected to act "uncompromisingly as a professional organization when it comes to the job." The *ikko nagashi* production system is about more than just making excellent products. It also entails conducting inspections between processes and taking responsibility for defective items resulting during manufacturing. A professional attitude is also an absolute must because Metrol's products must be accurate to one-thousandth of a millimeter.

No need for an administrative department

Metrol has only one person each assigned to administrative areas like human resources, general affairs and accounting. Department managers in charge of sales and production sites carry out employee reviews. Metrol believes these managers can treat personnel more fairly because they are the ones who know their workplace better than anyone else. Front-office employees take charge of general affairs. These workers may play two or three roles each. When somebody has to make a business trip overseas, no approval form is required. Plus, they are given a credit card for their expenses. There is a verbal understanding about the responsibilities involved. The company relies on experts like lawyers, tax accountants and labor and social security attorneys for subjects requiring their specialized knowledge, such as law, accounting and social insurance. That is why one person is sufficient to take care of each of these back-office tasks.

Company founder Akira Matsuhashi was a first-generation developer who built a groundbreaking endoscope at the end of his time working for a major camera maker, but the management that resisted the development and granted him little in the way of public recognition was the beneficiary of his work. Akira was a firm believer in the business philosophy that "at a manufacturer, a bloated back office stifles developer creativity." For a long time he used interviews and other conventional methods for hiring new workers, but many of them could not adapt to the company's free-spirited culture and Akira was acutely aware that this system did not illuminate an applicant's true capabilities. Now Metrol conducts interviews in the presence of an expert in psychological analysis. This has made the hiring process more expensive, but it has produced a visible result in that the company can now identify workers who will soon perform well after being hired.

Metrol also has operations overseas in China, India and Taiwan, but their purpose is not manufacturing but sales. The locally hired staff in these countries are recruited for management positions and are given decision-making authority. In other words, they are treated just like the Japanese employees. Metrol has websites and posts advertisements in English, Chinese and other languages and now does business in over 60 foreign countries. Most export deals are settled in Japanese yen. Metrol has taken a different path from larger firms and other SMEs to stay in business. Its goal is to be a highly creative company and it harbors no aspirations to be a big enterprise.

Spotting a product from 20 years ago before anybody else

Hyogo, one of Japan's 47 prefectures, is known as a mountainous area. It is also home to OHCHI NURSERY LTD. The business is located in a rural district within the city limits of Tamba, albeit far removed from the central part of town. The factory is surrounded by fields and a stream of fresh water flows near the premises. Noise

Employees perform manual tasks at an Ohchi Nursery production site

pollution and foul odors are nowhere to be found. Unless told otherwise, many people probably have no clue that a factory is located out here. At this production site set amid a wealth of natural surroundings, Ohchi Nursery makes dried flowers and preserved flowers. The company has a large share of the dried flower market in Japan. Ohchi Nursery is also a top player globally, with exports of preserved flowers to such destinations as America and China and a worldwide market share of over 30%.

Preserved flowers have the long-lasting properties of dried flowers, along with an enduring lushness and the scent of a freshly picked flower. The biggest selling point for preserved flowers is that they pretty much remain just as fresh as a flower bought at a florist. In all the processes involved in delivering flowers to consumers, from picking and production to preservation and shipping, Ohchi Nursery utilizes the original techniques and knowledge the company has learned. This is an enterprise with the potential to further increase its global market share.

Ohchi Nursery leaped to global prominence in the niche market of preserved flowers 20 years ago when then-managing director (and current company president) Tadashi Ohchi traveled to Western countries to purchase roses and other blooming plants for producing dried flowers. During that trip, he came upon preserved flowers at a German flower market. He could immediately tell that "they are no different in appearance and feel from freshly picked natural flowers. They also retain a fragrance and I thought they have the potential to replace dried flowers and take the market by storm." He added, "I still can't forget the impact that moment had on me. My heart was racing." Ohchi also made a decision he felt sure of: "I knew there would probably be difficulties involved, but I decided to make preserved flowers our company's next leading product."

The founder of Ohchi Nursery was Tadashi's father, Masaichi Ohchi. Soon after completing compulsory education, Masaichi took an apprenticeship under a master flower arranger. In his 20s he went independent by opening a flower shop in Shinchi in Osaka. During World War II, air raids devastated the streets of Osaka. Unable to make a living, Masaichi returned to his family's home, which was near the current location of Ohchi Nursery's factory. Continued bad fortune only made matters worse, as a traffic accident hospitalized him for nearly three months. His son, Tadashi, said, "My father fell on really hard times back then." We can easily imagine that his family was doing everything they could to get by. But Masaichi would overcome these travails. Although his injury limited his physical abilities, Masaichi still had his brains. He came up with the idea of turning wild mountain ferns into dried flowers.

It took Masaichi about half a year to make a product ready to ship, but his dried flowers, which he bleached and re-colored, got wrapped up in a boom that extended beyond Osaka to other major Japanese cities like Tokyo and Nagoya. When he expanded his lineup of dried flowers, Masaichi expanded his sales network throughout the country and by the 1960s he was exporting abroad. The flowers were also well-received in overseas markets. Masaichi grew his business into the biggest dried flower company in the world, with a 50% share of the global market. The smooth sailing would not last forever, though, as the Nixon shock removed pegged exchange rates for global currencies like the Japanese yen and the U.S. dollar, while the oil crises of the 1970s added fuel to the fire. The Japanese currency had been fixed at 360 yen to the dollar, but it rapidly appreciated and skyrocketed beyond 200 yen to the dollar.

SMEs that relied on exports for a heavy proportion of sales were hit hardest by these events. Many went bankrupt by export prices that fell by around 50%. Oil price hikes by the Organization of Petroleum Exporting Countries (OPEC) struck yet another blow. The dried flowers that were Ohchi Nursery's main product later came under attack by foreign imports into Japan. If the company had taken no action, it might have followed in the footsteps of the many SMEs that fell into decline due to the high yen and ballooning oil prices and perhaps there would be no Ohchi Nursery today. However, as president of the company, Masaichi played the appreciating yen to his advantage. Because the currency's gains meant that he could buy imported unprocessed flowers more cheaply, he began processing these for sale in Japan. That is how the company survived.

Tadashi, the current president, already had a sense that preserved flowers, which garnered little attention 20 years ago, would be a huge product that would replace dried flowers. There is little doubt that he was very much influenced by how the company used knowledge and ingenuity to get through the changes that occurred in these trying times...to say nothing of growing up watching his father, an intrepid entrepreneur, turn the tables and actually grow his business.

Taking full advantage of SME strengths

When Tadashi returned from his journey to the West, he embarked on a project to develop preserved flowers. One of the advantages of an SME is that the head of the company can meet face-to-face with users and business partners to get vital information that can determine the future of the enterprise. If Ohchi Nursery were a large company that delegates procurement of unprocessed flowers to lower-level employees, then it is possible that information about preserved flowers would have never reached Tadashi—and even if it had, other companies may have beat him to the chase and developed preserved flowers first, thus robbing him of the chance to turn them into a new business. Another advantage of an SME is that the leader's decisions can be quickly transformed into action. Large companies and even medium-sized enterprises spend needless time deciding on their policies and there are numerous cases of this weakness ruining incredible business opportunities. But the president of an SME is almighty. President Tadashi claims that his company "does not consciously transition to action so quickly," but Ohchi Nursery is a model example of how SMEs that achieve great growth in fast-changing environments run their businesses.

Ohchi Nursery did, however, experience a series of hardships while developing its preserved flowers. There were already companies in other countries that were making this product, but all of them kept their production methods secret. The only thing Tadashi knew about the process was that osmotic pressure is used to remove the moisture from the flower and replace it with a chemical substance that keeps the plant as lush as a freshly-picked specimen. The key techniques, such as what chemical substance replaces the moisture and how it is sucked out of the plant, was not public information at all. Without the techniques and the expertise, Ohchi Nursery had to reinvent the wheel, conducting research and development entirely from scratch. The R&D team examined numerous sources as it sought a chemical substance to replace the moisture and groped in the dark trying to figure out how to suck out that water. This situation remained static for some time. A year after the team had begun its R&D project, it had not yielded any results. It was still the same story after two years of work. The only thing the team had built up was piles of useless flowers discarded after experiments.

It would be a lie to say that the team was not racked by doubt and uncertainty. The team wondered whether continued research would actually create preserved flowers. But Tadashi would not give up. Perhaps he could have been happy with increasing profits from dried flowers and the fact that the company was financially sound. A more powerful force, though, was the pride he took in the voluminous techniques and knowledge about dried flowers that the company had built up. After three years of R&D, Ohchi Nursery was still far from done, but the company had produced something resembling a preserved flower. It was a woman named Keiko Sakaoka who did it. She was a through-and-through flower fanatic. After graduating with a degree in life science from the department of science at the Himeji Institute of Technology (now the University of Hyogo), Sakaoka "wanted to work with flowers," so she took a job at Ohchi Nursery, a company of only 100 or so employees. She took advantage of the opportunity to conduct tests with beakers, gradually scaling up to containers that allowed for small-scale production.

Sakaoka planted the first seeds of the project's success. She said, "My achievement was a coincidence arising from how I was absolutely absorbed in my research, which stemmed from my love of flowers and the fact that I know they aren't made in most places of the world." But her explanation that she "made my discovery by accident" is probably just her being humble. There are many great discoveries in the history of science that were happened upon by chance. In most cases, however, the discovery only came after the researcher poured their heart and soul into their work and conducted repeated experiments thousands, tens of thousands or even hundreds of thousands of times. Likewise, we would do well to consider Sakaoka's success as the fruits of extensive effort in which she applied the fullest extent of her expertise.

However, turning a complex plant like a rose into a preserved flower proved to be difficult with Sakaoka's technique. This is a problem because what the company most wanted to make into a preserved flower was roses, which are in higher demand than any other flower. To develop a viable process, the company formed a project team of employees who were former biology majors. One person was permanently assigned to Bangkok, Thailand, where roses are produced, to speed up the development work. It took nearly three years, but eventually the team was able to maintain the flower's characteristically delicate, soft petals and make a preserved rose just like one that blooms in a garden. This accomplishment satisfied the requirements for entering the preserved flower market.

In the first step of making a preserved flower, one uses alcohol and other ingredients to extract the moisture from a procured flower. Next, the alcohol is replaced with oil, fat and other substances. The flower then undergoes further processing before final inspection. This may sound like a simple job, but most of the work is performed by hand. Of course the very first step of picking the flower is a manual task, but flowers undergo subtle changes as the day passes from morning to afternoon and then evening. Because a flower is most lush and beautiful in the morning, workers try as much as possible to pick them at this time. A flower can also be affected by the season and the day's weather. Damaged or deformed flowers cannot be sold. A worker must also pay attention to how the flower is blooming before deciding to pick it. Ohchi Nursery procures flowers from Japan only when they are in season.

The company imports the roses that are its prototypical product from south of the equator. These roses grow in the highlands of Kenya, Colombia and Ecuador, at altitudes of between 2,500 and 2,800 meters. When it is April in the northern hemisphere, these roses are picked and transported to Japan. Ohchi Nursery chose these areas because their extreme daytime temperature variations make for the most beautiful of roses. Hydrangeas are another popular flower. Ohchi Nursery uses hydrangeas from the New England region of the United States because of their uniquely shaped blossoms. Gypsophila, pulled up along with their five-meter roots, are imported from a semi-arid region of the Rocky Mountains. Ohchi Nursery's orchids, which are characterized by their smaller size, are picked in Thailand, thus taking advantage of local geographical features. The company imports 10 million roses alone each year, but each and every one of them, even the smallest of the lot, are handled with great care.

The secret behind a huge market share

In addition to roses, Ohchi Nursery deals in hundreds of varieties of preserved flowers. Pink roses come in a range of shades, from light to dark hues. There are even different designs and sizes. The company is constantly increasing its lineup. For example, it has recently expanded beyond flowers by commercializing *hiba* cedar for use as Christmas trees. Prices also vary widely, from relatively inexpensive flowers costing 300 yen a piece, to pricier items that sell for as high as 1,800 yen each. When Ohchi Nursery started up its preserved flower business, it was impossible for them to make large flowers, but it can now produce large roses and hydrangeas in a vast array of selections from the affordable to big-ticket items. Meanwhile, quality control and customer service are the things the company pays attention to in the greatest of detail.

Before shipment, experienced employees conduct rigorous checks on color, shape, weight and other qualities for each and every item. During these inspections, they look particularly closely at color, shape and apparent volume. No matter how well an item may qualify as a flower, if its appearance suffers because the color is poor, the shape is even slightly deformed or the weight is low, it holds no value as a product. The veteran workers involved in the inspections meet once a week to make sure everyone is applying the same criteria. Inspections are tough work requiring many years of accumulated experience. Meanwhile, inspectors must remain vigilant lest they let down their guard and allow otherwise unacceptable colors or deformed shapes to ship out to customers. Of course, judging apparent volume is a subjective endeavor. To help maintain objectivity, inspectors will gather to double-check their standards for shape, hue, apparent volume and other criteria and work toward being on the same page. Their goal is to prevent inconsistent quality and keep any defective products from being overlooked.

To enable speedy shipments, Ohchi Nursery has a large distribution warehouse and a centralized management system employing barcodes. The distribution warehouse maintains a constant temperature and humidity in order to deliver fresher flowers. Customers have recently stopped maintaining inventory and ask that Ohchi Nursery send only the quantities they need when they need them. The company has responded to this request by building a streamlined management system capable of next-day delivery to most regions of Japan, excluding some areas such as Okinawa and parts of Hokkaido and Tohoku. Everything from picking the original flower to delivery of the final product is carefully done by hand, one flower at a time. This is likely the biggest reason why Ohchi Nursery has maintained the largest share of the global market.

Components that set international standards

Nikkohm Co., Ltd. is a manufacturer of resistors, which play a vital role in electrical equipment used in a wide array of fields including power, automobiles, traffic lights and trains. Unlike other resistor makers, Nikkohm makes unique products that no other company can replicate. These products are high-performance industrial resistors that can withstand demanding conditions for use in power, automobiles, medical devices and more.

When the Great East Japan Earthquake struck on March 11, 2011, 19 of the 27 bullet trains in Tohoku were running above normal operating speeds, but a seismic detection system applied the brakes to slow down the trains before the seismic waves reached the tracks. All the bullet trains came to a full stop within two minutes after the system detected the impending shaking and no passengers or crew were injured. This performance was lauded for demonstrating the advanced technology of the Japanese Shinkansen. A large electronics manufacturer made the braking mechanism and that mechanism used Nikkohm resistors.

The best example of the company's advanced technological prowess is the Multi-Junction Thermal Converter. This component is used in measurements that determine standards for power transformers. Using American-made thermal converters was once the norm, but Nikkohm was able to compare the root mean square (i.e. effective value) of direct current and alternating current with an incredibly accurate sensitivity of 0.00001%. Nikkohm now monopolizes the market.

The result is that Nikkohm's components set voltage standards in countries around the world. There are around 200,000 manufacturers in Japan, but few of the components they make take measurements that are used around the world as international standards. The fact that an SME from the city of Misawa, Aomori Prefecture could accomplish this is a remarkable achievement. This technology was created in a joint research project with the National Institute of Advanced Industrial Science and Technology (AIST) in Tsukuba, Ibaraki Prefecture.

Nikkohm has produced thermal converters that have been used in a wide range of thin-film thermocouples. As thermal converters have limited applications, they are by no means a product that sells in large quantities. However, the company's policy espouses a "duty to continue making an item so long as customers who purchased it continue to exist." Even though Nikkohm cannot sell most of these products anymore, they still appear in the product list on the company's website. Meanwhile, when AIST viewed the Nikkohm website as the institute was developing a next-generation standard for alternating current using superconductive Josephson junctions, it saw that Nikkohm was quite capable of providing the best precision in the world.

Before becoming president of Nikkohm, Shigeru Hidaka earned a degree from the school of science and engineering at Japan's National Defense Academy, after which he worked at the National Institute for Defense Studies and a private-sector laboratory. As a researcher with a doctorate in engineering, Hidaka long held a grand dream of developing an advanced product that would be used worldwide.

When Hidaka combined his ideas with Nikkohm's store of knowledge, they developed a thermal converter that would set the global standard for alternating current. Since most users of thermal converters are laboratories and universities, it is not a product that the company can expect to yield much in the way of earnings. However, the main buyers of this product have all been institutions from around the world that set national standards for alternating current. In addition to Japan's AIST, they include the U.S. Department of Commerce's National Institute of Standards and Technology (NIST), the Standards Council of Canada (SCC), Standards Australia, the Thai Industrial Standards Institute (TISI) and the Polish Committee for Standardization (PKN). Nikkohm's thermal converter gained global attention as a perfectly accurate component after the company jointly presented a research paper with AIST at an international conference. The company was flooded with email inquiries from people in other countries who learned about Nikkohm from international research papers. This helped the company build up its business thereafter.

Too groundbreaking

Among the power resistors that are the company's leading products, its industrial 900-watt, 300-watt and 200-watt power resistors have won particularly high admiration for using some of the best technology in the world. With each model, Nikkohm utilizes advanced techniques to imbue the resistors with good discharge characteristics and thermal stress capabilities and to maintain a high level that nobody else can keep up with. For example, Nikkohm's thin-film metallic resistors have a resistor tolerance (a measure of resistance precision) of 0.01 and a temperature coefficient of resistance (the resistance-change factor for each degree Celsius of temperature change of the resistor) that is one part per million for each degree Celsius. Both of these numbers are some of the best in the world. As mentioned earlier, resistors are used in a wide range of fields and they are indispensable components for electrical devices that supply energy. This means that without resistors, we would be unable to produce electricity or to send the power we generate to homes, factories or anywhere else. From televisions, refrigerators and other typical appliances in your home, to traffic signals on the road and train control devices used to operate the Shinkansen and other rolling stock and more recently in the fields of automobiles and medicine, resistors have a vast range of applications.

Resistors range in price from inexpensive models costing a few dozen yen each to pricier items that cost several thousand yen a piece because they are equipped with advanced technology. Nikkohm specializes in high-performance industrial resistors needed for advanced technologies in areas like charging equipment for electric vehicles and hybrid vehicles, power transmission for electric companies, train control for the Shinkansen and smartphone base stations.

Resistors are often used under demanding conditions with high temperatures or humidity, in extremely low temperatures, or in situations where electrical flow can spike at any time. Resistors are also used on our roads, in the traffic lights we benefit from every day. These resistors must last for 30 or 50 years, even in the rain or snow. They must also operate in places like Hokkaido, where the temperature can drop to -40°C or lower in the winter, as well as on hot city streets where the heat island effect can raise daytime temperatures in summer to over 40°C. Even under such challenging conditions, Nikkohm's resistors perform admirably.

One area where resistors help save lives is medical devices. An MRI machine uses magnetism to scan the brain and other parts of the human body. It requires instant jolts of power and you can find Nikkohm resistors in this equipment, too.

When Nikkohm developed its resistors, they weighed less than one-tenth what their conventional counterparts did and possessed capabilities several times better. Even so, when Nikkohm put them on the market, hardly anyone bought them. The irony was that because the resistors were so advanced yet so small, users did not believe they would perform as promised. Later on, when an American company came out with a similar product, Nikkohm finally won users' trust and the resistors began to sell well. Despite the happy ending, it was not an amusing episode for Nikkohm.

The addition of electronics in automobiles and the production of more light-weight vehicles did a lot to grow the market. In the hybrid vehicle market, where parts need to be compact and light, more than half the resistors used are made by Nikkohm because automakers want to take advantage of their weight, which is less than 10% that of a conventional resistor.

Return from the verge of bankruptcy

Eventually the banks Nikkohm dealt with ceased altering the terms of debt repayment and the company was pushed to the verge of bankruptcy, but the Japan Finance Corporation for Small Business (JFS)—now the Small and Medium Enterprise (SME) Unit at the Japan Finance Corporation—extended a hand to help with the restructuring. In talks on rebuilding the company, the JFS showed Hidaka a corporate turnaround plan written by an SME revitalization support council. Under this restructuring scheme, Aomori Bank would provide new financing so that Nikkohm could fully fulfill its debts to its old primary bank with a lump sum payment. The new financing by Aomori Bank would come with backing from a credit guarantee association so that even if Nikkohm became unable to repay the loan, Aomori Bank would not be stuck with the debt. Furthermore, the proposed turnaround plan included financing in the form of a corporate revitalization provided by the JFS Aomori branch.

After solving the country's financial problems, Hidaka followed the advice of the JFS to narrow down Nikkohm's business to the industrial resistors that were the company's core technology and to proceed with developing new products in this category. Another basic part of this turnaround plan included using IT to carry out more international business deals directly. To pay for the development of new products, Nikkohm made full use of resources such as R&D grants for creating new technology, provided by the Ministry of Economy, Trade and Industry (METI), and R&D grants for local industrial technology offered by Aomori Prefecture. Resistor manufacturers generally fall into one of two groups: companies that use mass production to ensure profitability and manufacturers who make special, advanced products one at a time. However, Nikkohm successfully remade itself from the ground up into a company that makes advanced products one at a time, in great variety and with medium-sized production operations. Nikkohm currently deals with 250 companies worldwide and its business ranges from versatile resistors used in traffic lights and power generators to advance resistors found in the field of nanotechnology, a bleeding-edge industry.

An 80% female workforce

Nikkohm follows the customary Japanese business practice of periodic hiring to recruit engineers at a certain time of the year. The company has also remodeled unused facilities to build an engineering wing where engineers can get technical development support. Another secret behind Nikkohm's ability to build a strong engineering team comes from excellent scouting of talent. More than a few of the engineers the company gets to know through academic conferences and networking events have reasons to move to northern Japan, where Nikkohm is located. Some feel compelled to go back to their hometown in Aomori Prefecture because their parents are getting old, while others want to raise children in a pleasant environment with natural surroundings. These are the kinds of engineers Nikkohm tries to nab. The company uses more than academic background to evaluate a candidate, but says that "graduates from top universities also find jobs with us."

Nikkohm's management say that "our highly skilled engineers and our female employees are the foundations of our company." In fact, 80% of the company's workforce is female, of whom half are part-timers. There are two reasons why these part-time women produce unique products that are some of the best in the world. One is that these employees are also allowed to operate production equipment. Nikkohm makes nearly 100% of its production equipment in-house. One reason why is to prevent the company's secrets and knowledge from leaking out to rivals, but another is that to make machinery that these female part-time workers can use to manufacture products after only a month or so of training, the equipment has to be simple to operate and extremely safe. All these employees are enrolled in Employees' Pension Insurance, Unemployment Insurance and other such programs. They can also take paid time off for childbirth and childcare, which on average four to five people use in any given month. The husbands of many of these part-time women also work, so sometimes they have to take a day off for an entrance ceremony or sports festival at their child's school or because their child suddenly fell ill. When this happens, the other workers find a way to make sure things continue to run smoothly at the factory.

Nikkohm has a three-scale personnel evaluation system that assesses employees on such qualities as proficiency and motivation, for which workers may be rewarded. The company also meets one-on-one with each person to provide feedback on their evaluation. There is a recruitment system for every position, from part-time to permanent roles, and Nikkohm hires several people a year. Special bonuses are paid in summer and winter. Due to the rules in the Japanese tax code, working spouses among the part-time workers incur disadvantages when annual income exceeds 1.03 million yen or 1.30 million yen. However, almost all of Nikkohm's part-timers work enough hours to earn more. Apparently, "the only difference between a permanent employee and a part-timer is that the former have administrative and training jobs, while the latter only perform work that suits them." Female employees at Nikkohm are treated just the same as their male counterparts. This is likely one of the driving forces behind the company's growth.

A story of both a business and a technology

KOHOKU KOGYO CO., LTD. is a company of around 110 employees with its headquarters located in the city of Nagahama, Shiga Prefecture. Its primary line of products is lead terminals, which are critical components of aluminum electrolytic capacitors. These capacitors are essential parts found not just in automobiles, but also in solar power generation equipment, telecommunication base stations and liquid crystal televisions. Kohoku Kogyo is the undisputed leader in this field, with a dominating worldwide market share of around 40%, but it is a relatively unknown global company. Its history is synonymous with the history of how human civilization has developed better and better lead terminals. Kohoku Kogyo has also developed an entirely original optical fiber component that has a global patent. This SME is a company eager to venture boldly into new businesses.

To put it simply, a capacitor amasses a store of electricity, like how a dam amasses a store of water. That makes capacitors some of the most crucial parts within the components found in electronic devices. In addition to digital TVs, uses for capacitors have recently expanded to green technologies such as solar power generation, telecommunication base stations for smartphones and more. Capacitors can vary in their usage, materials and other properties. Some types include plastic capacitors, ceramic capacitors and electrolytic capacitors. An aluminum electrolytic capacitor can store a large amount of electricity and endure high levels of heat. A lead terminal plays the role of guiding electricity stored in a capacitor so that it flows to a circuit board or other destination. Without a lead terminal, a capacitor cannot function. As the top company in the world producing these vital components, Kohoku Kogyo contributes to society in both the business world and in the lives of regular people.

Kohoku Kogyo-made lead terminals for aluminum electrolytic capacitors are important components that guide discharges of electricity stored in the capacitor to a circuit board or elsewhere. The terminal itself comprises an aluminum wire, a lead wire, a pressed part and a welded section. To produce a lead terminal, Kohoku Kogyo cuts the aluminum wire, welds the lead wire with the aluminum wire after the latter has gone through a chemical process called anodic oxidation, presses with a mold, then performs washing and further chemical treatment. This description may give the impression that the manufacturing process is a very straightforward one involving incredibly simple materials, but the truth is the opposite. First of all, most of the lead terminal materials have an extraordinarily small diameter of only microns. The aluminum wire serving as the raw material is not your typical low-grade variety. Kohoku Kogyo uses aluminum wire with a high purity of 99.92%. Rare, expensive aluminum like this is not used in other industrial products.

Therefore, Kohoku Kogyo custom-orders this aluminum wire from large steelmakers. The chemical treatment of the aluminum wire forms an oxide layer that exerts a large influence on the flow of electricity. This treatment is performed at the same time the aluminum wire is welded to the lead wire. The treatment has a major effect on capacitor production processes and quality.

It takes 0.2 seconds to produce each lead terminal. In one minute, 300 are welded. The actual time required for welding is 0.004 seconds. It must not take any more time than this, but if the welding were sped up it would hurt quality and make it impossible to configure the weld with the desired precision. Four steps are performed during the full 0.2 seconds: pre-welding, position verification, discharge and then push-forming the lead terminal into shape. Under a watertight quality maintenance system, workers use monitors to watch over the steps involving electrical current and the push-forming. Customers can select from three weld configurations: the standard type, a bowl-shaped weld and a cone weld. During pressing, unprocessed rounded bars can be rolled, cut or shaped to make the product. Pressing the aluminum parts is such a very quick job that 300 shots can be performed every minute. Kohoku Kogyo can also provide users with the pressed shapes they desire, such as a double stamp, edgeless, four rounded corners, or a deburred shape.

The processes mentioned thus far include advanced techniques and know-how that other companies cannot reproduce, but the greatest of them is the washing, in which Kohoku Kogyo uses an alkaline detergent. It washes off excess material and any oil or stains that adhere during the manufacturing process. This washing may seem like a simple job, but Kohoku Kogyo's washing does more than remove oil, as the alkaline detergent also etches the surface of the rolled aluminum to form a subtle pattern of indentions on the pressed aluminum surface. This reduces the aluminum foil's contact resistance, thus improving capacitance. The patterned indentions formed by the etching are only nanometers in size. Moreover, although normal dielectric withstand is typically 200 volts, Kohoku Kogyo has enhanced its engineering prowess so much that the company can make lead terminals capable of enduring high voltage of 500 to 750 volts.

Designing technology for 20 years in the future

Conventional lead terminals for aluminum electrolytic capacitors are made with lead or tin plating, but the discovery that products containing lead can harm the environment or cause a product to deteriorate resulted in the phasing out of lead in Europe under the Restriction of Substances Directive. Now the lead wires there are tin, not lead. But with the lead removed, the tin in the part of the lead wire that is welded to the aluminum will recrystallize over time, thus creating protrusions called "whiskers" that are only microns in diameter. These whiskers can cause a capacitor to short-circuit, or create a failure in an integrated substrate that makes the product malfunction. In order to solve this problem, a plastic coating can be applied to the weld, as it will keep oxygen separate from any moisture, thus preventing the aluminum from oxidizing and corroding.

The plastic coating solves the problems associated with the environment and product deterioration. However, since the plastic employed is susceptible to heat and physical shocks, concerns arise if the lead terminal is used in a place where it is likely to be bumped, or where high humidity can create problems due to the moisture and temperature. Kohoku Kogyo develops lead terminals that do not flake, crack, scratch or otherwise incur damage. To ensure this, the company conducts tests. The physical endurance test subjects a lead terminal to 4,000 cycles at two temperature ranges: -55°C to 105°C and -40°C to 85°C. In the humidity test, a lead terminal goes through 4,000 hours at 85°C with 85% humidity and at 60°C with 95% humidity. The temperature test runs the lead terminal for 1,000 hours at 150°C.

Kohoku Kogyo put so much effort into developing this lead terminal with plastic coating because it expects it could be a capacitor component in the next-generation auto parts that will require greater safety in the green cars of the future. The company is improving its engineering capabilities with its eyes set on five, ten, twenty years from now. That looking ahead to the distant horizon to develop technology is part of Kohoku Kogyo's culture.

Shojiro Ishii, the father-in-law of the company's current president, established Kohoku Kogyo at its current location back in 1959. The enterprise has built lead terminals for aluminum electrolytic capacitors ever since, but it has never taken a day off from taking on the challenges of technology.

President Futoshi Ishii said, "I've heard that there were times when we struggled to pay our employees or couldn't avoid laying people off." But even when Kohoku Kogyo confronted serious business difficulties, the company never relented in building up its store of technology and knowledge. Although at the time of its founding Kohoku Kogyo did not have a special, high-end offering like many other companies had, it did eventually earn the respect of the industry for products forged from technology and expertise no other firm can replicate. Most of the machinery operating here was made in-house. Those machines may cost more than purchasing something from elsewhere, but apparently, making high-quality products would be impossible with somebody else's equipment. Even those devices Kohoku Kogyo buys from machine tool manufacturers are "in effect made by us" because it custom-orders them and packs them with its own technology and know-how.

Driving out the cheap, shoddy rivals

In addition to engineers with a passion for developing technology and experienced, knowledgeable employees, Kohoku Kogyo benefits from the presence of young workers to whom these assets are passed down. No matter how cutting-edge the technology used to manufacture the excellent machinery operated at an SME production site, the skill and speed with which an experienced employee handles it is completely different when an unfamiliar set of hands takes control. Likewise at Kohoku Kogyo, an unacquainted young worker will not be as fast as a veteran even at initial response of the machine. This gap occurs when a machine has been imbued with the company's multitude of knowledge. The explanation from Kohoku Kogyo is that "our company's products are made with advanced engineering and expertise no other company can imitate." That is what saved the company and made it the business that it is today.

Manufacturers in countries like South Korea and Taiwan began making the same products as Kohoku Kogyo's in the late 1990s. The biggest weapon these companies had was a cheap product made with cheap labor. Although they could not compete with Kohoku Kogyo in terms of performance or quality, with prices they held a decisive upper hand. In many instances they used this advantage to enlarge market share and steal away Kohoku Kogyo's customers. Futoshi was appointed president during these trying times. Long-time customers were saying they "want to use Kohoku products, but the price difference was too big so they asked us for discounts." In many of its dealings, the company started having to offer reduced prices. It was a difficult decision to make and even so its market share dropped from nearly 50% down to a number in the 20s. Kohoku Kogyo had become embroiled in such a fierce price war that there was no guarantee it would remain a going concern for this long.

In a few years, however, the cheap prices from foreign competitors underwent a massive change. Taiwanese, South Korean and even Chinese manufacturers who had enlarged their share with low prices experienced soaring wages and production costs. Meanwhile, demand for high-performance, precise, high-quality lead terminals began to grow in advanced industries like electronics and automobiles because the cheaper lead terminals failed to perform adequately. There were also problems with the quality and precision of the cheap lead terminals and customers came to realize that, as the saying goes, "You get what you pay for." This shift forced some of the non-Japanese manufacturers who had hawked low-priced products to go bankrupt. Some lead terminals may be made by companies in other countries like China and Malaysia, but Kohoku Kogyo has won by following a policy of competing on quality and performance with advanced products made in Japan.

Research on par with the big boys

And now Kohoku Kogyo has a new main product to follow its lead terminals for aluminum electrolytic capacitors: optical fiber parts. It is a business that is already turning a profit. To use more precise terminology, the company is making components for makers of optical communication modules, such as optical fiber arrays and multi-hole capillaries and ferrules. Optical fibers are important tools for transmitting information because they can send and receive massive amounts of data. Optical modules connect to nodes in these networks such as data centers and mobile phone base stations. They also serve as components in long-range transmission equipment. For example, optical modules connect submarine communications cables for making international phone calls to cable landing points. Kohoku Kogyo makes parts used in these modules: light power monitors that measure luminosity, optical splitters and WDM fiber arrays that bundle and partition optical signals, optical attenuators for controlling optical strength and optical isolators for directing light. All these components are manufactured with ultra-fine fabrication working at the nanometer scale.

Kohoku Kogyo has also been successful in developing a method for producing a special optical fiber called a photonic crystal fiber. This fiber is made by opening 90 holes in a fine strand of quartz fiberglass with an external diameter of 126 microns. It is very effective at keeping light contained and enables non-linear optical control. Kohoku Kogyo has also made it possible to mass-produce microcapillaries. These can be used as capillary tubes with six tiny holes 100 microns in diameter cut into a fine square of quartz glass. This product is sold for applications in analytical equipment used by medical laboratories. Currently it is mostly used for research purposes, but this product has great growth potential due to anticipated future demand in medical equipment. Annual sales of these new products have risen to above 1 billion yen. "We've made them completely profitable."

These new products apply completely different technology and are used in completely different fields from lead terminals. Since the time of Shojiro Ishii, Kohoku Kogyo has been exploring the frontiers of engineering. The company has been tackling challenges in new fields since its earliest days, but now President Futoshi Ishii is dedicating serious resources, as exemplified by his efforts to recruit experts with PhDs in materials engineering.

Despite being a firm of some 110 employees, Kohoku Kogyo has such a great research team that when its members go to America or elsewhere to attend an academic conference on engineering relevant to the company's business, they not only collect information, but also present their findings in English. Despite being a small group, this is a level of research on par with large companies and it has allowed Kohoku Kogyo to succeed at expanding from the ultra-advanced field of nanotechnology to enter into medicine, which is expected to be one of the industries of the future.

It is imperative for all companies, including the big ones, to develop great new products that will keep the business going on into the next generation, but this task poses a greater level of difficulty for SMEs. Even so, Kohoku Kogyo is one of the few enterprises that is successfully developing those next-generation products.

An essential part of the global automotive industry

Ohara Jushi Kogyo Co., Ltd. based in Nagoya, Aichi Prefecture, makes auto parts out of plastic. These parts help a vehicle move, stop, turn and burn fuel. Most people never see them, but they require incredibly high precision and quality because they make cars safe and protect human lives. One of these is a small, rectangular plastic part only two or three centimeters long, but without which an automobile engine would not run smoothly, fuel efficiency would plummet and its exhaust would contain more hazardous substances. Despite the company's small size, its parts, which an automobile cannot do without, are found in around 53% of all automobiles produced worldwide. Ohara Jushi may not be the only maker of these parts, but it has a dominant global market share. That means if its supply of parts were cut off, global automobile production would come to a standstill. The name is not well-known, but the company possesses a hidden might.

The most distinctive thing about Ohara Jushi is that the numerous parts it makes are related to most of an automobile's many functions.

For example, Ohara Jushi makes parts for gas pedals, which help a car move. People usually don't see them. One part is the rubber section of the part that meets the driver's foot, while another is mounted to the engine to control its revolutions. The gas pedal has come to play a greater role since most recent automobiles have automatic transmissions. Many of these pedals are made from plastic or metal; Ohara Jushi's part is the former.

If the brake pedal does not consistently bring the car to a stop, then a person will not feel safe riding it. The Ohara Jushi brake parts that help a car stop filter out impurities in brake fluid so that it flows cleanly. This is a critical part, as the brakes may cease to work if impurities contaminate the brake fluid.

Ohara Jushi parts also helps vehicles and their components turn: bearing seals inside the steering column; other bearing seals for windshield wipers; and internal parts for power steering. Ohara Jushi parts have never been recalled for having a defect.

This SME has nearly a thousand types of products and, depending on the product in question, makes nearly 200 to 300 million of each every year. Some of these may be unique parts that no other company in the world makes, while others are the best of their kind, but the one that helped Ohara Jushi secure a tight grip over more than half the global market and rise to the undisputed pinnacle of its business sector is a material used in parts for burning fuel: a hydraulic control seal made from polyphenylene sulfide (PPS) plastic. A hydraulic control seal is installed inside an engine. It is a small part, with a diameter of two to three centimeters and a thickness of only few millimeters. Fitting an engine with the seal improves combustion efficiency. It can also reduce the amount of hazardous substances in the exhaust. It is a very simple item: a rectangular board of plastic that has been processed in several places. As a critical engine part, however, it must pass strict criteria: the four corners must be at a certain angle, with a margin of error of only 0.05 millimeters. Furthermore, because the PPS plastic used to make it is 30% potassium titanate, a large amount of gas is emitted during the fabrication process and shaping the material poses a serious challenge.

Foundations of the auto industry

One thing that many of Ohara Jushi's products have in common is that they are mass-produced based on drawings provided by customers; Ohara Jushi has no departments for product development or design. This is possible because auto parts makers and unprocessed plastic manufacturers have achieved advances in automobiles and plastics while accumulating expertise on plastic molding and molds. In the process, they have developed reliable techniques for mass molding products with high added value. This is true for hydraulic control seals, a market where Ohara Jushi retains the largest share in the world. In the 1950s, then Bank of Japan Governor Hisato Ichimada publicly disparaged the passenger vehicle industry. At that time, Japanese-made passenger vehicles paled in comparison to foreign cars in terms of performance, quality and price. As Governor Ichimada personally believed "it's impossible to cultivate a domestic automobile manufacturing industry in Japan," he instructed the bank to not provide financing to automakers. There were also likeminded lawmakers in the Diet. Practically forsaken by everyone, Japan's domestic automobile industry grew anyway. Today Japan is one of the world's leading producers of automobiles, which are renowned for being fuel-efficient, safe and reliable, but the country faced a string of difficulties on the way to this lofty position. This story also tells the history of how the Japanese took on technological challenges, refusing to let the world beat them.

Automobiles are a huge industry, as each vehicle is assembled from over 20,000 parts, which means auto parts makers also play a major role in this business. Together, car makers and parts makers have built up what is today's automotive industry. Making even the smallest of parts that most people never even see is the product of cumulative innovations. SMEs that have created some of the leading products in the world have contributed to Japan's development into one of the world's greatest car-producing countries and these enterprises continue to support that industry. Ohara Jushi is a model example of such a company.

Meanwhile, the Japanese automobile industry has experienced major changes in terms of the materials used to manufacture products. Up until the early 1970s, Japan's petrochemical makers sought economies of scale, lowering costs through massive output. However, the oil crises of the 1970s swiftly robbed these companies of their international competitiveness. To survive these circumstances, Japanese petrochemical makers developed engineering plastics with superior strength and resistance to heat and wear. These plastics are suited for parts and components in advanced industries like automobiles, machine tools and aircraft.

In those days, the use of plastics had already spread to everyday household items. As machinery and automobile parts, however, their use was limited, such as in seats and other interior elements. But the chemicals industry developed a series of new engineering plastics usable for key automobile parts. The engineering plastics in production range from general-use types like polycarbonates (PC) and polyamides (PA) to high-performance super engineering plastics such as polysulfone (PSU), polyarylate (PAR) and polyphenylene sulfide (PPS). Today they have a diversity of applications in cars: exteriors (roofs, door handles, windshield wipers, wheel covers), interiors (seatbelt buckles, interior light covers, headlight cleaners) and engines and other structural elements (various control units, engine parts, power seat gears). The big chemical makers are even working on research with the aim of having plastics replace metal to account for the majority of parts in car frames.

Unique technology and knowledge

Automakers who want to produce excellent cars have a bond with the plastic manufacturers working on the cutting edge to create the likely vehicle plastics of the future. Ohara Jushi played the role of forging that bond. The company's auto parts, including the hydraulic seals found in most of the world's vehicles, are in widespread use at automobile plants. But if the task of developing the latest technologies and components were left only to the makers of auto parts and plastics, then Ohara Jushi probably would not have become a world-leading parts manufacturer. The company possesses a wealth of engineering to facilitate steady mass production that rivals cannot imitate, along with a store of knowledge taught to the employees who carry out the most important role in fabricating finished products. This is the decisive difference that makes Ohara Jushi stand out from other makers of auto parts and plastics.

Like many plastics manufacturers, Ohara Jushi has created its products thanks to the skills of veteran workers who utilize their years of experience and honed intuition. The company, reliant upon the abilities and instincts of these valuable employees, has used scientific methods to develop its production techniques. This is how Ohara Jushi quickly grew into the global leader of a niche field.

When engineering plastics first came into usage, Ohara Jushi was a typical company in this field, as its polyacetal (POM) was heavily utilized in the Nagoya area. The firm already possessed advanced technologies from the early days of engineering plastics, but continued to enhance them thereafter. When I asked for more details I was turned down. "We can't talk about that," I was told, as this information is a company secret. Suffice it to say that Ohara Jushi has unique technologies and knowledge relating to the mass molding of super engineering plastics.

Take, for example, controlling the amount of moisture in the raw material. High-performance super engineering plastics are in a completely different league from regular plastics and although there are different varieties, what they are all certain to contain is water. The greater the quality of a super engineering plastic's functionality, the more it is affected by moisture. Inevitably, the amount of water content will cause subtle changes to properties such as hardness and molding precision. If Ohara Jushi delivers a defective auto part, it could cost a person their life. Raising accuracy to within one-hundredth of a millimeter requires near-perfect controls, beginning with the unprocessed plastic. The company used to rely on the experience and intuition of veteran employees, but later switched to a method of measuring and controlling water content. Under this method, a sample is heated and then the resulting water vapor is made to react with a reagent of calcium hydroxide. By measuring the moisture content, Ohara Jushi can plot the curve along which the plastic dries. This allows the company, at any time, to arrange for mass production of a product within a pre-determined moisture content range.

Furthermore, unprocessed plastic will go through cycles of water absorption and drying due to changes in the external environment, such as temperature and humidity. Ohara Jushi prevents unprocessed plastic from absorbing water or drying by using it immediately after opening its container, or by allowing experienced employees to use their skill and intuition to make adjustments. To check and monitor temperature and humidity where the plastic is stored, the company uses thermometers and hygrometers that automatically record readings. According to Yoshinori Ohara, the company's president, "The water inside the plastic material can experience slight alterations not only from the day's temperature and humidity, but also from changes in the weather, like rain, clear skies or clouds." The material can also develop deviations depending on whether it is placed in the center of the storage area or kept in a corner. Therefore, it is important to keep thermometers and hygrometers running at all times and monitor conditions constantly so that the company can store the material under appropriate conditions and ready it for use.

In the past, Ohara Jushi had to rely on experienced employees who were masters of their profession. While the company still values passing on the skills of such personnel, it has also developed a proprietary method for steady mass production by visualizing and analyzing such things as plastic temperature and molding conditions. Ohara Jushi worked with a machine tool maker to create the necessary machinery for steady mass production. These machines are designed to turn out products when operated by any employee who has received the proper training. Melting plastic used to emit gases or cause machines or molds to break down, but Ohara Jushi succeeded in developing a way to prevent emissions and vastly improve the performance of its molds and machinery.

The company took a series of steps to bring the cost of products down to a relatively low level. President Yoshinori Ohara says his company has established a production method that enables it to adequately compete against foreign rivals with cheaper labor. He adds that this is possible because this method turns out products free of defects by improving consistency, even for mass-produced items, and by maintaining consistent manufacturing output. The company currently has a production center in Vietnam, but hopes to bring costs at its Japan plant down to a comparable level. Ohara Jushi plans to set up another overseas production site in the future, but not because it is looking for cheap labor. Rather, a declining population in Japan means the domestic market will not expand, so the company intends to make manufacturing a worldwide operation. Ohara Jushi was founded by Toshio Ohara, the grandfather of the company's current president. It started out as a painting business, then went into plastics processing and later pivoted to manufacturing. Toshio's son and the company's next president, Masao, used engineering plastics to turn Ohara Jushi into an auto-parts company. His son, Yoshinori, is now growing the business into a global one by pushing into new, more advanced technologies.

A Japanese monopoly in the fading semiconductor industry

Japanese semiconductors once swept the globe, but today the competition in South Korea and elsewhere has caught up and many of the big semiconductor manufacturers have closed their plants in Japan. They were forced to lay off a large number of employees, as their glory days were but a memory of the past. If we take a look back at history, we see that it was heavy industry that led to Japan's postwar economic boom that began in the 1960s. Advanced industries, principally electronics and automobiles, took over in the 1980s as the leaders of the Japanese economy. By the late 1970s the semiconductor business replaced steel to establish itself as what the Japanese call "the rice of the industrial sector." From the late 1980s to the early 1990s, Japan boasted awesome semiconductor production capacity that accounted for more than 50% of the global market.

It was from this time onward, however, that Japanese semiconductors rapidly lost competitiveness. Global market share dropped to 28.5% by 2000. And it did not stop there, as it has currently fallen to around 14%.

Although Japanese companies have a smaller share of the semiconductor market and their more prosperous past has faded into memory, there are still quite a few areas within the semiconductor business where Japanese firms are still fairly dominant. Many people in the industry say that Japanese semiconductor companies still have enormous influence.

Let's use photomasks as an example. They are integral to the manufacture of semiconductor devices. A photomask is a glass plate to which a circuit pattern has been transferred. Polishing this plate requires a seemingly advanced technology and expertise and Japanese companies account for the lion's share of the global photomask market. The global leader in the business of polishing recycled plates is Chichibu Denshi Corporation, an SME headquartered in the city of Chichibu, Saitama Prefecture.

During semiconductor processing, laser light is fired at a circuit pattern that has been drawn onto a glass plate. This laser burns the pattern onto silicon or another material. This glass plate is like the negative film used in photography. In the past the circuit patterns that were etched were fairly simple, but technological advances have allowed for the inclusion of more complex patterns. Photomask production technology has progressed in step with these advances. Since this photomask polishing and cleaning would not be possible without highly advanced technology and knowledge, Japanese companies have a monopoly on this business. They say that if something happened to bring production in Japan to a halt, then that would be the day the global semiconductor industry comes to a standstill. Japanese companies hold the key to the highly integrated semiconductor business.

Despite being an SME, Chichibu Denshi occupies a corner of this market. One can see how respected the company is by its inclusion in the "100 Japanese SMEs Garnering Global Attention," a feature printed by the Japanese edition of influential American magazine *Newsweek* (Nov. 14, 2007). The *Newsweek* article gives Chichibu Denshi's photomask polishing techniques very high marks: "Japan has a monopoly on the production of the photomasks needed to manufacture the semiconductors embedded in electronic devices, but this is the only company that specializes in photomask polishing. It receives numerous requests to polish used products from overseas companies who recognize the company's greatest technological prowess."

"The biggest reason why our products are what they are is our vast knowledge."
When polishing a photomask, microscopic blemishes and dust must be kept close to zero. Furthermore, the photomask must have an overall flatness with variation of only microns. With the degree at which integrated circuits have been miniaturized today, even particles of dust or dirt that are microns in diameter can, by themselves, cause serious problems when printing a circuit. Items made from scratched, dusty or dirty photomasks are worthless as commercial products. A manufacturer using such photomasks would accrue massive losses. Polishing a photomask that is free of dirt and scrapes is by no means a simple task. Apparently, a small photomask with an area of 6 square inches that has ten or more scratches 0.1 microns in size (1 micron = 1/1,000th of a millimeter) cannot be shipped as a product. Photomasks go through a manufacturing process requiring incredible precision of 0.1 microns, or 1/10,000th of a millimeter.

Just because a photomask is unscratched does not mean it will pass inspection, as the total surface must have a gap between high and low areas of no more than 1 micron. Hard materials such as diamonds are used for the polishing. Each photomask goes through multiple polishing procedures. During the many steps, polishing is performed with relatively large diamond grains at first, then gradually transition to finer materials on a four-level scale. After the completion of each step the abrasive employed becomes smaller. Chichibu Denshi's polishing machinery was custom-ordered from a machine tool maker. The design was based on input from the SME's experienced employees. However, the photomask manufacturing process involves more than merely placing materials in a machine that then spits out a finished product.

In addition to abrasives, polishing requires chemicals and other special materials. Chichibu Denshi must rely on veteran workers' many years of experience and intuition in order to properly blend the chemicals and add them at the correct time and in the right amounts. One slip-up alone can affect the product's performance. The intuition of experienced personnel is also needed to make the fine adjustments to the machinery's rotational speed and pressure. Chichibu Denshi President Takahiko Suneya said, "We rely on a fair amount of engineering, but the biggest reason why our products are what they are is our vast knowledge." As he says, the foundation of the company's photomask polishing business is the knowledge of ultra-precision polishing the long-time workers have accumulated.

Creating a new market inaccessible to big companies

A fine example of Chichibu Denshi's numerous achievements in advanced engineering would be its water purifiers. Regular water has an electrical resistance of zero ohms, but for cleaning this company uses water with 18 megohms of resistance, which blocks nearly all electricity. In addition, the removal of calcium and other chemical substances, as well as bacteria, dirt and other foreign matter makes this water nearly 100% pure.

Chichibu Denshi's infatuation with imbuing products with ultra-fine accuracy begins with its precision polishers, but is best embodied by the microscopic defect sensor. This equipment is used to identify infinitesimally small scratches and other flaws. It is operated in a special cleanroom. This room has a cleanliness that would normally be unthinkable elsewhere, as it has only one 0.5-micron particle of dirt per 30 square centimeters. The microscopic defect sensor, used in the final inspection phase, symbolizes the company's focus on ultra-fine precision to the very end.

Chichibu Denshi has prevented its rivals from keeping pace with its recycled photomask polishing business. The quartz used to make a photomask is expensive, so a single unit today still costs around 15,000 yen, which is certainly not cheap. Another thing to keep in mind is that a photomask that has been used once can still be polished back into brand new shape. Each photomask can be recycled in this manner four to five times. Chichibu Denshi possesses a dominant share of the global market for photomask recycling that is 50% to 60%. Of course, this is a niche market when compared to the market for new photomasks. And because it is a niche market, as President Suneya explains, "Big companies won't get into this business because they don't foresee a profit. That's the only reason why we are lucky enough to be the global leader." However, larger firms have not been holding back so much as of late.

We all know that a big company will intrude in a field where SMEs are doing business if it sees the chance for even a small profit. And it is still quite common for the larger enterprise—when it cannot manufacture the product in question on its own—to bring the SME under its wings through an M&A or other such use of enormous financial muscle. The small size of the photomask recycling market is not the only reason why big companies have not entered the business: they have given up on the idea because Chichibu Denshi uses its advanced technological prowess to provide this service to users affordably. Being a niche market alone does not keep out bigger players. What keeps them at bay is the fact that Chichibu Denshi was the one who created this market and it designed it so larger companies could not get in on the game.

Acting as a normal company would have spelled doom

Chichibu Denshi sees its next big businesses as being in silicon carbide (SiC) and gallium nitride (GaN). These compounds are garnering attention as next-generation materials for building power semiconductors because they experience little loss and boast excellent resistance to heat and pressure. But their greatest trait is that they have half the electrical power loss that conventional semiconductors do. In addition of course to the power transmission sector that delivers electricity to homes and businesses, demand is expectedly to soar in fields like hybrid vehicles, solar power generation and air-conditioning. However, working with materials Chichibu Denshi had not handled in its photomask business meant that developing the technology came with numerous difficulties. In particular, because both silicon carbide and gallium nitride are incomparably harder than normal materials, the diamond polishing techniques the company has formulated over many years were not up to the task. Cleaning methods also differed from those Chichibu Denshi had been employing.

To overcome these obstacles, the company made clever use of publicly available funds from sources such as the Japanese government's strategic basic technological advancement support program; the METI manufacturing, commerce and services grant; and the Saitama Prefecture grant to support businesses entering next-generation industries. Thus Chichibu Denshi came nearer to establishing the new technologies involved. The Japanese government and local administration provide grants systems like these for new technologies and new businesses with the goal of modernizing SMEs and helping them to grow. The way Chichibu Denshi skillfully utilized these subsidies to seize a fresh business opportunity could serve as a model for a new SME business strategy.

Chichibu Denshi's origins go back to 1962, when Takahiko's grandfather built a factory for silk products. This was the traditional industry of the Chichibu area. Silk farming, or sericulture as it is otherwise known, had previously been a major industry here and at this time Chichibu had a huge concentration of silk businesses. Later, however, when Japan began importing cheaper products from abroad, the silk business' prospects dried up, even in Chichibu, and entered a period of decline. To survive, Suneya's company went into the transistor sector. Using this electronic technology as a foothold, the company acquired knowledge from large manufacturers and entered the photomask business. This was the beginning for the Chichibu Denshi of today.

Takahiko, the current president, earned a degree in electronics and communications science from the Faculty of Science and Engineering at Waseda University. He then took a job at Nippon Telegraph and Telephone Public Corporation (since renamed to NTT). At that time, the company had a program for sending young employees with promising futures to America to study. Japan's telecommunications industry lagged far behind America's, so the goal behind having these workers learn in the United States was to train the company's future executives. The study abroad program produced some of NTT's most important figures, along with others who left to build their own big information and communications firms. Takahiko was picked to attend two years of college in America. Had he stayed at NTT, he probably would have become an executive. He said, "I knew that I was on a comfortable career track at NTT and I never once thought about taking over the family business."

Takahiko's father, however, pressed him incessantly about becoming the company's next leader. At first Takahiko adamantly refused, but eventually he gave in and started working at Chichibu Denshi. Soon after becoming the president, he entered a trying period of his life. It was around this time that technological advances had made it possible to embed large amounts of information on a single photomask. The result was that once buoyant demand for photomasks nosedived to less than one-third their peak. Chichibu Denshi was rapidly losing business. The company had faced business crises in the past, but Takahiko did not take the situation lightly. He coordinated an urgent response that included the formation of a sales project team to market goods and services to potential corporate buyers. The company ended up surviving its greatest challenge yet. The lesson learned then: "Companies that don't have strong technological capabilities cannot survive." If Chichibu Denshi had acted like a normal company, then it would have been caught up in a price war that would have led to a sudden drop-off in business once a recession hit. The company has resolutely enhanced its engineering prowess out of the conviction that SMEs without this asset will not make it.

It is because of this lesson learned during hard times that Chichibu Denshi, despite being the global leader in the recycled photomask polishing business, is directing all available resources toward developing novel semiconductor-related products with new materials like silicon carbide and gallium nitride. The company is fully supportive of employees who want to learn new skills and improve themselves, because much of Chichibu Denshi's business relies on the expertise of employees and the electronics industry is evolving day-by-day. Most people would probably assume that a company that polishes photomasks for producing semiconductors would have a mostly male workforce. However, Chichibu Denshi values its female employees so highly that Saitama Prefecture has recognized the company as a gold-star business that "supports employees' work-life balance and has put into practice efforts to create a workplace environment where women can thrive in their jobs."

Chapter 5

Winning with "Business Category Changes" that Capitalize on Expertise

Four Companies, Including One that "Will Not Move the Operational Core to China"

Corporate bankruptcies climbed to around 19,000 a year during the worst period, but have now almost halved to around 10,000. However, 99% or more of the companies that fail are small- and medium-sized enterprises (SMEs). There are also a lot of SMEs that use these situations to their advantage and overcome crises by embarking on "second launches" that substantially transform their existing business categories. This chapter profiles companies that have successfully undertaken a second launch and are at the top of their fields worldwide or aim to be. One thing common to these companies is that rather than shifting to completely different types of industries, they are evolving technologies and expertise cultivated over many years, and making them sources of new businesses.

Technologies and expertise that even major manufacturers cannot imitate

ANTEX CORPORATION (Minato Ward, Tokyo) is a leading manufacturer commanding a share of over 40% of the global market for large slewing bearings, which are core components of hydraulic excavators and the other construction machinery used on construction sites on a daily basis. Construction sites may face fierce heat of over 40°C, or conversely be assailed by intense cold of below -20°C. Frequently the working day lasts over 12 hours. Even hydraulic excavators used for general purposes have gross weights of 20-28 tons. Even when the excavators are sitting idle the slewing bearings come under loads of between 15 and 18 tons, but when they are being used to dig holes or demolish buildings the principle of leverage comes into play between the bucket at the tip and the work assembly, so the load increases to as much as 300 tons. In the case of large, special hydraulic excavators the gross weight can exceed 800 tons in some cases, and when operating the loads can easily exceed 1,000 tons. They use super-large bearings about four meters in diameter. Antex is trusted worldwide for slewing bearings that operate with millimeter-level accuracy when working, regardless of the type of bearing, large or small.

Antex's large slewing bearings

The mechanization of today's construction sites is progressing. They are becoming modernized workplaces where cranes and bulldozers play active roles. Antex's large slewing bearings are also used on such construction sites. While they are also used in cranes and other machinery, they are predominantly used for hydraulic excavators. Hydraulic excavators are extremely popular as construction machinery, to the extent that if small excavators of a few tons are included, there are virtually no construction sites where they are not in use.

Antex's large slewing bearings

Hydraulic excavators are composed of the self-propelling portion enabling the excavator to drive to the construction site itself, the small room that the operator climbs into to operate the machine, and the bucket and the arm-like working assembly that moves it. The operator's small room and the hydraulic excavator's series of core components for the bucket are mounted on top of the self-propelled machine, and when the excavator is operating they move as one. It is not just the machinery doing the work that moves; an excavator is constructed so that the upper part of the self-driving portion all rotates as one, through 360 degrees. The components linking all that together are the large slewing bearings made by Antex.

In longer cases the arm-like working portion can be around 10 meters in length, and unless the bearings move accurately, the excavator's working point will become quite clumsy, making it impossible to demolish buildings and houses or move away earth and other material accurately and efficiently. Bearing diameters range from one meter to as many as four meters for particularly large bearings, and according to Antex's works manager, Yasunori Ueda, "including Antex, even worldwide there are only a handful of companies capable of manufacturing highly precise slewing bearings in sizes this large."

Although the large bearings Antex manufactures are one variety of bearing in the wider sense of the word, major bearing manufacturers do not actually make them. The biggest reason why Antex, an SME, is a leading company worldwide is that it possesses abundant technologies and expertise other companies cannot imitate. Another reason is that it boasts an integrated production system that begins with cutting the raw materials and ends with an inspection using a three-dimensional measuring machine. Large slewing bearings are composed of an outer ring, inner ring, a toothed gear, outer ring mounting holes, inner ring mounting holes, a plug, a plug stopper, rubber seals and so on. Of these components, the only ones Antex does not make itself are the bearings' steel balls and the seals.

Operational core will not be moved to China

Making large slewing bearings begins with selecting the raw material. Because the bearings operate under severe conditions, ordinary steel material cannot cope. Consequently Antex uses a specially-ordered steel material produced exclusively for the company's use. The first task is to cut the steel that forms the raw material according to the size of the bearing to be manufactured, but at this stage the material is cylindrically-shaped. After this is heated to a temperature of 1,200°C, a press and several rolls are utilized to open a hole, and by widening this inside diameter, a ring of around one meter in diameter is formed. This manufacturing method is known as the ring rolling mill process. It is a unique technology that Antex developed, after repeated setbacks.

The ring is formed by rotating it while employing a forging method, but unlike the conventional method there is very little noise or vibration, a technology that other companies cannot hope to copy. Antex's plant received "environmentally-friendly" awards from Ibaraki Prefecture, where the plant is located, and the Ministry of Economy, Trade and Industry (METI). The unique machine, which Antex describes as "the culmination of all our company's technology and expertise," can handle every possible order, from high-mix low-volume production through to high-volume production. The experience and intuition that the employees working there have built up over many years are a major part of this ring rolling mill operating process. The employees adjust the speed of the machine up or down while monitoring subtle changes in the color of the material, which is heated to a bright red. Without the skills of highly-experienced employees, producing high-quality products would be impossible.

Once the roll forging is completed, the ring goes through a heat treatment process that gives rise to the forging raw material, and this undergoes a process to give it large "teeth," a process known as gear cutting. The accuracy of the teeth is high, reaching one-hundredth of a millimeter. This then undergoes induction hardening to further increase its surface hardness. In the next process, holes for connecting the moving undercarriage to the main operating body are drilled on both the inner ring and outer rings. If these holes are too big, slackness will develop and render the excavator useless as construction machinery. Conversely, if the holes are too tight, assembly will not be possible. These are more than just holes – they employ an ultrafine processing technology.

That processing is carried out on a machine that is packed with the company's expertise and technologies, and was custom-built by a machine tool maker. Through an additional cutting process, cutting again takes place to improve precision, but at this point also, the accuracy is in units of one-hundredth of a millimeter. After the finishing machining, the bearing is assembled. The assembled bearing is sent for inspection. Only bearings that make it through a preliminary check and a durability test to check their weight and whether they can endure powerful forces during excavator operation, and then pass a final inspection employing a 3D device, are shipped. Most slewing bearings are large bearings with diameters exceeding a meter, and some reach diameters of three to four meters, but Antex enjoys a growing reputation for this exacting work.

Antex's Takahagi Plant in Ibaraki Prefecture is its main plant and where the majority of its bearings are made. In 2004 it established Antex (Shanghai) Corporation, a wholly-owned manufacturing company in Shanghai, but the Chinese subsidiary only undertakes machine processing after forging, induction hardening and the assembly process. Forged items are made at the Takahagi Plant or procured locally. The subsidiary mainly ships to Japanese construction machinery makers that have set up businesses in China and India, and foreign construction machinery makers with plants in Europe.

Antex began producing in China as its trading with foreign companies increased. Domestic construction machinery makers have advanced into China in succession, and Antex's decision to enter China was partly due to demand from these trading partners. To a considerable extent then, rather than proactively entering the China market, Antex's relationships with its trading partners inside and outside Japan left it with no choice but to do so. And while it will increase production in China due to those considerations, it does not intend to shift the core of its operation, the ring rolling mill division, to China.

Forward-looking capital investment

Antex is capitalized at 50 million yen and has a workforce of 250 people. In some years annual sales exceeded 12 billion yen, but are currently around 8 billion yen. It is also a company with a history, having been founded in 1917. Originally, it was a sole proprietorship set up in Fukagawa, Tokyo by Kumagoro Ando, great-grandfather of the current president, with the goal of manufacturing and distributing forged products. Kumagoro appears to have been blessed with a talent for business. In 1937 he relocated to Haneda in Ota Ward to expand the operation, and his company began manufacturing mainly optical instruments and other equipment as an army-controlled plant. In 1941 he sought to start the organization anew as Ando Iron Works, an unlimited partnership. With the end of the war, military demand-related work disappeared, so Kumagoro quickly turned the company to peacetime production of equipment such as internal combustion engines, vehicles and transport machinery.

Most of the employees who remember that era have passed away, so we can only surmise based on documents and other materials, but eight years later, in 1949, Ando Iron Works undertook a capital increase and reorganized as a publicly-incorporated company. A further four years later Kumagoro's son Shichiro became president. Although it remained a small company for some time after the war, given that the plant received certification from Lloyd's Register QA in 1958, it was definitely using its sophisticated technologies to steadily expand its business achievements. In 1965 the company successfully developed the ring rolling mill that forms the basis of today's Antex. This triggered a major transformation at the company. It was around this time that the current chairman, Haruo Ando, joined Antex. He recalls that at that time the company had no ambitions whatsoever of becoming a maker of large slewing bearings.

Demand for construction machinery gained momentum in the 1960s, but around that time Antex was simply a subcontracting manufacturer that supplied bearing makers with components for slewing bearings for construction machinery. Large manufacturers that specialized in bearings and whose main sources of orders were automobiles, machine tools and other equipment took on large slewing bearings for construction machinery single-handedly also. However, even though they are all called bearings, the bearings used in automobiles and machine tools are completely different in nature and manufacturing approach to the large slewing bearings used in construction machinery. Consequently the fact was that "it was not a field that large bearing makers were passionate about." Neither were they about to embark on developing the kind of slewing bearings that construction machinery makers were seeking.

On the other hand, just as construction machinery makers' demands for outstanding slewing bearings were increasing, the Ministry of International Trade and Industry, as it was then known, came out with a plan to develop the construction machinery industry. Antex, at that time a components maker, "was contacted about manufacturing bearings for construction machinery, and embarked on development," explains Chairman Ando. Thanks in part to technical cooperation from bearing makers, construction machinery makers and other companies, Antex successfully developed the ring rolling mill that could be described as the foundation of the company. This led to its subsequent advances.

That is not the only reason why the company has grown so big today, however. In 1980, in anticipation of an expansion in construction machinery demand, Antex fully relocated its entire production division from the Haneda Plant, which had grown cramped, to Takahagi City in Ibaraki Prefecture, where its main plant is currently located. Furthermore, in 1982 it also relocated the production division at Rokugo, Ota Ward, to the Takahagi Plant, transforming the plant into an integrated facility handling everything from materials through to machine processing.

This temporarily meant the company was carrying excess equipment, but because it was able to respond to the subsequent growth in demand from the construction machinery industry, in time it provided the opportunity for the company to develop into a global manufacturer. Proactive capital investment has become a company tradition, and it continued to expand thereafter also, adding a fully automatic ring forging and heat treatment production line and constructing the Takahagi Plant No. 2 and Takahagi Plant No. 3.

The company name was also changed to the present Antex in 1992. The "An" comes from the "An" in Ando Iron Works, "tech" was added as a nod to the corporate culture of emphasizing technology, and the final "x" denotes a sense of growing into the future.

In 2017 Antex will celebrate its 100th anniversary. In light of that milestone, a project team composed of current President Yohei Ando and young employees is beginning to explore what the next 100 years will hold for the company. Key items they are planning to consider include lifting the company's sales to over 10 billion yen to reflect the company's 100 years since being founded, developing new demand for large slewing bearings, and furthermore, advancing into new fields where this technology is applicable. The technology is already being used in wind power generation, and it will undoubtedly be possible to cultivate new demand in renewable energy and other fields. The company will continue to take on new challenges even in fields where sophisticated technologies are currently being applied, on the basis that ample potential to cultivate new operations exists.

The construction machinery industry experienced a severe decline in demand of close to one-third as a result of the financial crisis. Antex was also affected by this development. A backlog of orders somehow allowed it to stay in the black in 2009, but the following year it posted a major deficit for the first time since its founding. Nevertheless, the company's hidden strength enabled it to return to the black in 2011 and remain profitable since. The essence of that strength is its world-class, sophisticated technological prowess.

Survive as an independent company, rather than become a subcontractor for a major manufacturer

Takabayashi Mfg. Co., Ltd. is an SME headquartered in Kanazawa City, Ishikawa. It is capitalized at 25 million yen, and including part-time staff it has a workforce of 85 employees. The company manufactures hydraulics components for industrial machinery, construction machinery and other equipment, and even domestically it is said to possess top-level technologies for hydraulics components. If this was the company's only strength it would be just one of many blue-chip SMEs that exist in the regions. Most notably, however, Takabayashi Mfg. has begun jointly producing aircraft components with a surface treatment company and a heat treatment company in Hokuriku. These three companies have partnered with a mid-tier trading company in Osaka to build a nationwide production network, and have already decided to embark in earnest on manufacturing a diverse range of aircraft components. This is more than just a new survival measure for SMEs – it offers the companies the potential to spread their wings globally.

Takabayashi Mfg. was established as a company for manufacturing components such as shafts for textile machinery by the grandfather of Managing Director Hideki Takahashi, who is effectively in charge of running the business on behalf of his uncle, President Kenichi Takabayashi. Subsequently the company worked on machinery components for precision machining, while also expanding its sphere of operations to include fields like machine tools. Takabayashi Mfg.'s advance into the field of hydraulics equipment for industrial vehicles and construction machinery, a field that now accounts for around 90% of its sales, was the result of it being approached by hydraulics equipment makers with proposals for it to make certain components. Ishikawa Prefecture is home to global construction machinery majors, so there is a tendency to assume Takabayashi Mfg. mainly manufactures components for these major construction machinery makers, but it is a completely independent company that trades with domestic and overseas construction machinery and hydraulics equipment makers. It is not a subcontractor for a specific manufacturing major.

From early on, rather than survive as a subcontractor for a specific company, "We placed an emphasis on strengthening our technologies in order to survive as an independent company, which in turn led to us having sophisticated technologies. Even now, I think our technological prowess is evaluated highly by many of our trading partners," explains Managing Director Hideki Takahashi.

A succession of independent SMEs, not just subcontractor SMEs, are changing fields or discontinuing their businesses, and amid this trend the SMEs that are able to survive have three options. If they have parent companies that have relocated their production bases overseas then they relocate their production bases overseas with them. Alternatively, they beat the competition by cutting their costs through intensive rationalization and mass production. Or, they preserve their competitive power by taking the outstanding technological prowess they already possess and enhancing it further. Takabayashi Mfg. succeeded by choosing the third path. And doing so presented it with the opportunity to make a new entry into a major market: the aircraft components industry.

To prevent costs from climbing and boost competitiveness

The Ishikawa Sunrise Industries Creation Organization (ISICO) was a major factor behind Takabayashi Mfg.'s entry into aircraft components. ISICO is a public interest incorporated foundation set up by Ishikawa Prefecture. It pursues initiatives such as new industry creation for SMEs and venture companies, start-up support and industry-government-academia cooperation. The scope of ISICO's operations are in fact very broad, covering everything from holding events and seminars to lending funding for capital investment, advising and assisting SMEs with advancing into overseas markets, holding exhibitions for cultivating market distribution routes in metropolitan Tokyo, and providing specialist advice on improving SMEs' businesses. By holding seminars and other events ISICO presents frequent occasions for local SMEs in Ishikawa Prefecture to come into contact with major companies from Osaka and Tokyo, thus promoting increased business opportunities.

Takabayashi Mfg. President Kenichi Takabayashi's association with Sumitomo Precision Products Co., Ltd. also came about at an ISICO seminar. Sumitomo Precision Products is a major precision machinery maker listed on the Tokyo Stock Exchange's First Section. It has annual sales of around 50 billion yen and employs some 1,500 people. Its core products include head exchangers and aircraft components, and within that, it boasts strengths in the landing gear used when aircraft land. Furthermore, it is placing an emphasis on expanding its business in the aerospace field, including successfully supplying the heat exchangers used for Airbus' state-of-the-art engines recently. With aircraft equipment, even a small defect is capable of triggering a major accident involving human lives. A high degree of accuracy and quality control is demanded for landing gear, heat exchangers and other equipment also, which in turn means outstanding components makers are required. Sumitomo Precision Products had been searching for a components maker with the ability to manufacture goods with precise accuracy for aircraft.

Meanwhile, although Takabayashi Mfg. makes outstanding components for construction machinery and hydraulics machinery, it had been looking to move into high value-added fields where its technologies were applicable and furthermore where high technological skills were required. The meeting between Sumitomo Precision Products and Takabayashi Mfg. is not simply a coincidence. Sumitomo Precision Products was hunting on a nationwide level for a components maker that possessed outstanding technologies and which it could build a relationship of trust with, in order to pursue expansion in the aircraft sector. Takabayashi Mfg. was looking for a foothold for entering growth industry fields by enhancing the sophistication of its technologies, and it had a growth-oriented spirit. It would be correct to conclude that the collaboration was a success for the very reason that it involved these two companies. Takabayashi Mfg. had been positioning components for construction machinery and hydraulics machinery as its core products, but due to the financial crisis its orders had fallen to close to 70% of what they had been up to then, compelling it to enter new growth fields. This too forms a backdrop to the partnership.

Takabayashi Mfg. began developing aircraft components from around the beginning of 2008. The following year, 2009, it supplied major aircraft components makers with hydraulic actuators (drive assemblies used for flight control systems) for aircraft. At that point it did not possess the technologies that are referred to as special processes, such as heat treatment, surface treatment and non-destructive testing, and so midway through the manufacturing process Takabayashi Mfg. sent the components to major aircraft component makers, which put them through the special processes and sent them back, a cycle repeated any number of times to come up with finished products. Because the back-and-forth journey taken by components resembles the jagged edge of a saw blade, this production format for aircraft components is known as a "saw-tooth" approach. To undertake the special processes work it is considered to be essential to acquire National Aerospace and Defense Contractors Accreditation Program (Nadcap) accreditation, which is mentioned later, but because few supplier SMEs have obtained it, the reality is that many large aircraft component makers have no choice but to adopt this "saw-tooth" production format.

Obviously this approach increases costs, however, and it also poses problems on the competitiveness front. That being the case, it was decided to utilize a next-generation fund established with contributions totaling 13 billion yen made by Ishikawa Prefecture and seven financial institutions, with the aim of being able to accept and produce orders involving all of the processes, coherently. Surface treatment company ASASHITA PLATING CO., LTD. (President: Hideaki Asashita) and heat treatment company FUKADA Heat-treatment Industry, Ltd. (President: Ken Fukada) took part in this initiative. Asashita Plating is an SME that is capitalized at 10 million yen and has 23 employees, but the company is highly-rated for the strength of its quality control and technologies, including undertaking general electroplating and carefully inspecting the quality after each process. Within that, it is considered to boast strong technologies in hard chrome plating.

Similarly, Fukada Heat-treatment Industry is an SME that is capitalized at 10 million yen and has 66 employees. Its main business is "tempering," which involves boosting the strength of steel material by heat treating it in its raw material state to improve its workability and organizational uniformity. The company also specializes in the advanced processing of steel material using approaches such as annealing and normalizing. 40% of its employees are qualified as metal heat treatment specialists, with five grade 1 heat treatment specialists and 23 grade 2 heat treatment specialists, another fact that demonstrates how strong the company's technological prowess is. Takabayashi Mfg. pursued a partnership with these two companies that boast sophisticated technologies because extremely sophisticated technologies and complex processes are required to produce aviation components.

Strict quality control is also demanded in the aircraft industry, and acquiring JISQ 9100, an aerospace quality management system certification belonging to the Japanese Industrial Standards (JIS), as well as Nadcap accreditation, are essential conditions. JISQ 9100 is a certification that was formulated by adding requirements unique to the aviation, space and defense industries to ISO 9001 certification. Similar certifications have been formulated in the U.S. (AS 9100) and in Europe (EN 9100). Additionally, JISQ 9100 was formulated by IAQG (International Aerospace Quality Group) accompanying the abolishment of the U.S. Department of Defense's standard specifications. They are quality management specifications covering companies involved in the aviation, space and defense industries. Furthermore, the information is also registered in a globally-common database system managed by IAQG, giving them an edge in customer order placements, and access to the global marketplace.

Meanwhile, for Nadcap a review is carried out by the PRI (Performance Review Institute), an administrative organization set up through the sponsorship of the world's leading aircraft manufacturers with the goal of ensuring the quality of special processes across the aerospace and defense industries overall. Acquiring JISQ 9100 (or AS 9100 or EN 9100) is a prerequisite, and it is classified into 17 categories, including non-destructive testing, chemical treatment, heat treatment, electronic devices and materials testing. It is necessary for a company to acquire certification in the special processing field it is in charge of carrying out, and for it to regularly renew its certification. The reviews are not document based in the sense of verifying whether or not arrangements are in place. Rather, they focus on practical aspects such as whether or not the company is capable of appropriately manufacturing products. Once quality manuals and relevant procedural documents have been translated into English there are also reviews in English. If items identified in reviews are not completed within 45 days and within four exchanges, companies are punished by having their accreditation suspended or cancelled.

Acquiring these two certifications are essential conditions for entering the aviation industry, even if it only involves making components. Takabayashi Mfg. acquired certification for non-destructive testing and surface enhancement, Asashita Plating acquired it for surface treatment, and Fukada Heat-treatment Industry acquired it for heat treatment.

SMEs combine collective strengths to establish "All Japan" framework

Special materials and unique processes exist in the aircraft industry to ensure safety. The representative example of a special material is super-high-strength steel. High-strength steel is used even in automobiles, but the super-high-strength steel used in the aircraft industry is almost twice as strong as the automobile steel. For a mainstream industry, the material is machine processed and then machine processed again after heat treatment. After undergoing finishing and then a grinding process, it is completed. By comparison, in the aircraft industry the process is identical up to the point of machine processing the material, but the steel needs to pass through 16 processes subsequently, including heat treatment, machine processing, stress relief, shot peening, finishing, grinding burn detection, non-destructive testing, finishing, chrome plating, grinding, processing and non-destructive testing.

Super-high-strength steel is hard, yet it is brittle like glass. It displays high strength when pulled, but its shearing strength is weak and it is vulnerable to metal fatigue. Additionally, after heat treatment a change in the organization of the steel material that is known as a "burn" is brought about, taking the temperature past the tempering heat using heat and other elements. Stress relief is a heat treatment for removing residual tensile strength, which negatively affects fatigue strength. Shot peening is a special process that is added to improve the steel's fatigue characteristics and enhance its longevity. This resolves metal fatigue and "burn." The above-mentioned steps are examples of the processes relating to the material, but finely-tuned specifications are also demanded during the grinding process, including the grinding fluid, the quality of the material used for the grindstone and its size and hardness, as well as the grinding machine cutting speed, the management of the grindstone's revolutions and so on. Not a single error can be allowed in any of the processes. That is the duty imposed on companies that are JISQ 9100 certified. There are also a large number of other inspection requirements, and unless a company passes all of them it cannot enter the aircraft industry.

Fukada Heat-treatment Industry, Asashita Plating and Takabayashi Mfg., together with YURA Sansho Co., Ltd., an Osaka-based general wholesaler of screws and nuts, set up JAN (JAPAN Aero Network) in February 2013. JAN brings together a large number of individuals who enjoyed long careers at aircraft makers. Drawing on their experience and contacts, the company undertakes consulting work from a comprehensive perspective, overseeing areas such as grasping global procurement trends, adjusting orders-received and drafting business strategy proposals. Nationwide, over 30 machinery component SMEs participate in JAN, many of them based in Ishikawa Prefecture. "Via Yura Sansho, which has a trading company function, it has been possible to establish a coherent 'all-Japan' framework of machinery makers nationwide to supply the world," explains Managing Director Hideki Takahashi.

Via JAN, in December 2013 the four companies realized a five-year long-term agreement with Sumitomo Precision Products. They deliver landing gear component units for Honda Jet, the small business aircraft developed by Honda Aircraft Company, and small aircraft made by Canadian aircraft manufacturer Bombardier Inc. The deal is understood to be worth about 600 million yen, so it is not a large agreement, but the fact that Japanese SMEs were able to form an alliance in order to deliver large quantities of aircraft components is a ground-breaking development. Furthermore, because JAN's core companies are concentrated in Ishikawa Prefecture and Japan is a narrow country compared to the U.S. and other countries, it has been able to keep its prices below those of U.S. components makers. Up to now, even though Japan's aircraft components industry is outstanding in terms of quality and meeting delivery deadlines, it has been considered inferior to Europe and the U.S. on the cost competitiveness front. However, JAN has been able to establish a framework that will enable it to lower its prices by around 10% in the future, ultimately allowing it to compare favorably with Europe and the U.S. in terms of cost competitiveness also.

Regulations on the aviation industry are being eased in countries worldwide. Low-cost carriers (LCCs) are seizing this as an opportunity to enter the market one after the other. Developments such as this mean demand for aircraft, particularly mid-sized aircraft with capacities ranging from 120 seats to under 170, will continue to grow. It is expected that demand for new aircraft alone will see the market expand to 32,000 aircraft and a total value of 410 trillion yen up to 2032. Centering on Takabayashi Mfg., SMEs in the Hokuriku region are attempting to make huge strides by collaborating to take on a gigantic global market whose proportions are as-yet unknown.

Switching business categories to participate in major global projects

Until only six years or so ago, Tonan Seiki Co., Ltd. (Anjo City, Aichi Prefecture) was a typical automobile components maker that generated 90% of its sales from automobile components, chiefly press-die and die-cast prototypes for Toyota. Today, however, automobile components account for 30% or less of its sales. In their place, it has achieved a transformation into an advanced company that undertakes cutting work on large nuclear fusion reactors, metallic molds for forged titanium parts that connect aircraft fuselages, and key parts for the medical equipment used in proton beam cancer treatment systems. Many of the products that Tonan Seiki makes are items brought to it by customers that have concluded Tonan Seiki is the only company left to turn to, after finding no other manufacturer in the world would accept their order on the basis that "it is not something we can manage."

It is a small company with a workforce of 50 employees, but it is also a blue-chip company that is taking on the world.

Tonan Seiki is participating in manufacturing key components for the International Thermonuclear Experimental Reactor (ITER) project. Simply put, ITER is a massive experimental reactor for generating the same type of energy on Earth as the sun. Following an agreement at a United States-Soviet Union summit meeting in 1985, in October 2007 an agreement by Japan, Russia, the European Union, the United States, India, China and South Korea to set up an experimental reactor officially entered into force. Kaname Ikeda, Ambassador to Croatia at the time, was appointed as the first director-general of the ITER Organization. The ITER is scheduled to begin operating in 2020, with the nuclear fusion reaction scheduled to take place in 2027. The facility will be built in Cadarache, France. The ITER plan is an international development project being implemented through international cooperation, and the participating countries account for half the entire world's population and around three quarters of its gross domestic product (GDP), so it could be described as a gigantic global project. Japan is performing an important role in this plan, which has a large number of settings where Japan's advanced technologies will shine. Japan will oversee the development of remote maintenance devices, heating equipment, measuring systems and other instruments in cooperation with Europe, the U.S., China, South Korea and the other participants.

These devices will be manufactured by major Japanese companies, but Tonan Seiki will oversee the processing of the 60 divertor cassettes, which are components in the nuclear reactor's core, and the toroidal field (TF) coils, which are similarly important components (total weight 1,300 tons). Stainless steel that is super-hard compared to ordinary steel material and which is highly adhesive is used in the reactor core, and Tonan Seiki will use machining to fabricate it. The entire reactor is over 14 meters high and close to 20 meters wide. The reactor core fits inside this and so is somewhat smaller, but there is no question it will be a massive structure nevertheless. Tonan Seiki will carry out the cutting work to micron level precision.

Tonan Seiki has also obtained certification to ASME standards, which conform to American nuclear power standards, for cutting work on nuclear power-related components. For the cutting tool, it uses equipment it developed itself, which it says makes it possible to cut hard materials slowly and cut adhesive materials as if shaving them with a razor. The company's unique technologies could not have come about without many years of experience and expertise. It boasts the world's leading technologies in this field and when the objects to be machined reach this scale, "We are the only company in the world capable of undertaking the work," explains President Shuichi Watanabe.

Promising product rivalling Toray's carbon fiber

Kobe Steel, Hitachi Metals, IHI, KHI and other companies set up Japan Aeroforge (J-Forge) with the goal of forge processing the titanium, nickel, ferroalloys and other metals used for aircraft, power plants and other purposes. Forging technologies that transform metals such as iron by giving them superior qualities have also become more sophisticated recently, and demand for them is also growing in fields such as aircraft components. These developments also formed a backdrop to J-Forge being set up. Forged metals have been used for armor, metal utensils and other items since olden times, and more recently it is anticipated that they will attract demand as aircraft materials. The aircraft industry is expected to enjoy strong growth of 4-5% per year from here on, and the number of manufacturers entering the field is soaring.

Obtaining forged components is a pressing challenge for heavy industry manufacturers, and Tonan Seiki also undertakes the making of metallic molds for the large titanium parts used in aircraft.

Furthermore, the Boeing 787 is attracting attention as an aircraft that has led the world in successfully lightening fuselages by using large quantities of Toray Industries, Inc.'s carbon fiber-reinforced polymers. Alongside carbon fiber, which Japan developed using a unique technology and which is viewed as a leading technology worldwide, another material that began being used in large quantities with the Boeing 787 is forged titanium aircraft parts, which like carbon fiber are light and boast an extremely high level of strength. Tonan Seiki is responsible for the metallic molds used for these forged titanium aircraft parts. The 787 encountered some problems temporarily, but it is considered to be an innovative aircraft, with demand anticipated to grow substantially in the future also. Metallic titanium and carbon fiber are viewed as being extremely compatible, and 787s are purported to use around three times the quantities used in conventional aircraft. In addition, Tonan Seiki has also received orders for products such as metallic molds for Airbus' landing gear. When it comes to these titanium metallic molds for aircraft components also, Tonan Seiki has few rivals, and the molds look certain to become a core product for the company.

One approach to treating cancer that is attracting attention at the front-lines of cancer treatment recently is proton beam cancer treatment. This approach is thought to significantly reduce the physical burden placed on the patient compared to a surgical procedure, making it possible for the patient to undergo cancer treatment without their everyday lives being unduly interrupted. This proton beam cancer treatment intensively irradiates a predetermined designated location with a proton beam while having virtually no impact on the normal cells surrounding the cancer lesion, thus attacking the cancer cells alone. Consequently, it is even possible to irradiate lesions that are close to vital organs. It is considered to display strong therapeutic outcomes for lung cancer, liver cancer, prostate cancer and other cancers.

A proton beam cancer treatment system consists of a cyclotron for generating and accelerating the proton beam, a beam transport system for sending the proton beam to the treatment room, a rotating gantry irradiation device for delivering the proton beam from any angle, and a device for taking x-ray images to determine the positioning. Of these components, the rotating gantry irradiation device is mounted on the rear side of the treatment room. It is an extremely large iron and steel structure 10 meters in diameter and weighing 120 tons. By undertaking the machining of this important component, Tonan Seiki has also made a major contribution to the development of proton beam cancer treatment systems. One reason why an SME like Tonan Seiki was capable of taking on the machining of what can be called a key component of medical equipment for an advanced treatment and succeeding brilliantly was that it had built up technologies and expertise in the course of designing and manufacturing large forged structures from the 1970s, when it was an automobile parts maker. Coupled with that, it also possessed advanced technologies in the field of designing and manufacturing accelerators that speed up charged particles. When manufacturing rotating gantries, pure iron is used as the raw material, but carrying out cutting work on pure iron is extremely challenging. Tonan Seiki's strength is that long years of experience have made it unrivalled in this field.

In addition to this, Tonan Seiki also takes on repairs and maintenance of large, specialty steel products that have been rendered unusable by cracks or abrasions. In some cases newly manufacturing these large products costs to the tune of several million or tens of millions of yen. However, thanks to a large repair furnace that the company introduced it is possible to repair them in a short space of time by taking advantage of preheating, heating and welding technologies. Tonan Seiki also develops one-of-a-kind technology products, including a machine that can drill holes in metal products accurately and to precise depths that it developed based on a subsidy for supporting product development by SMEs. Tonan Seiki "specializes in components that need a large truck to carry them" and require a high degree of precision, explains President Shuichi Watanabe, noting that "in more than a few cases these items cannot be transported without a trailer."

As mentioned earlier, another one of the company's strengths is "jobs that other companies have abandoned as hopeless." According to President Watanabe, "To survive, we took on things other companies turned down, and through desperate efforts we were able to complete them. It was through these repeated successes that we built up technologies and expertise." As a result, recently the company has been receiving a large number of orders from companies that have concluded from the outset that "If Tonan Seiki can't do it, no-one can." These strengths are underpinned by the skills and intuition of its highly-experienced employees, but because they will leave the company upon reaching mandatory retirement, the company has manualized their skills to ensure the technologies are passed on. This has made it possible to clearly see how far along an employee is in acquiring a technology, and systematically hand the technologies down to young employees too.

A welding department is vital for manufacturing large components, but because the work is carried out using high temperature gas or electric flame, temperatures in the workplace can exceed 40°C in summer. Because they are handling dangerous flame in high temperatures, and because sparks fly off at times, it is essential for workers to wear heavy-duty work clothes as well as special glasses that protect their eyes from the blue flame. In the past this was known as a "3K" workplace (*kitanai, kiken, kitsui,* meaning dirty, dangerous and demanding), and young people despised the job, but Tonan Seiki now has a welding team of six younger workers who carry out their daily duties while steadily honing their skills under the guidance of highly-experienced personnel.

While continuing to pass on technologies and expertise in this way on the one hand, Tonan Seiki also has a special project team consisting of selected employees. The team deals with new fields the company has not accepted orders from before and the manufacturing of products that require sophisticated technologies. Because these are "jobs that other companies will not take on," they call for originality and ingenuity, and a process of trial and error. Completing these challenging jobs through these repeated efforts enables Tonan Seiki to accumulate new technologies and expertise. These in turn lead to new orders. Tonan Seiki maintains that "the automobile field is an important business," but given the stage the company has reached now, it is no longer simply an automotive parts subcontractor. It is a niche player, but it is taking on the world.

Journey to becoming a global company

Tonan Seiki's current president, Shuichi Watanabe, is the one who took Tonan Tanko, a company his father Tomizo (now chairman) founded in Nagoya, and dramatically transformed it into the outstanding company possessing sophisticated technologies that Tonan Seiki is today. The company Chairman Watanabe established as a forging company was initially changed into a company manufacturing mainly metallic molds for Toyota, and its business performance was by no means poor. Nevertheless, the second president who took over after Chairman Watanabe switched to a sales approach based on securing orders through business entertaining, rather than positioning technologies as the sole selling point. This strategy failed, however, and the company's performance promptly deteriorated. Shuichi joined the company upon graduating from university and was a managing director at that time, but his direct opposition to the second president's business policies saw him leave the company. Employees also quit in succession. The business came to a complete standstill. Shuichi Watanabe was called back, and he returned as the third president.

But the company that awaited him was in a wretched state and a long way from its former glory. When he went to the bank to borrow funding he received a grim reception: the first thing he was told was "come and request a loan when you have finished paying back the money the bank has lent you so far." Turned down for a loan by the company's main bank, the company was pushed to the brink of bankruptcy. It was rescued from this crisis by a local credit union, Okazaki Shinkin Bank.

Initially, President Watanabe was told that borrowing money would be difficult, but the area manager at Okazaki Shinkin who supervised Tonan Seiki's area listened to Watanabe's business policies and other plans for three hours, and ultimately agreed to lend the company money on condition it reported its business performance each month. "Financial institutions of local residents and SMEs" is a business philosophy consistent throughout the credit union industry. More than a few credit unions collapsed as a result of straying from this philosophy during Japan's economic bubble era, but many remained locally-rooted and maintained sales as the main banks of SMEs. Luckily for Tonan Seiki, Okazaki Shinkin had been sticking to business that followed this "true path" of a credit union.

At the same time as Watanabe became Tonan Seiki's president, he utterly transformed the company's business policies, abolishing sales based on business entertaining across the board and striving to turn Tonan Seiki into a company that lives off its technologies. The first step was acquiring ISO 9001 and ISO 14001 certification. Following that, he radically improved the corporate culture in areas such as quality control and strict adherence to delivery deadlines. On that basis, it requested a threefold increase in the unit prices of its parts from Toyota's primary subcontractors. Although the threefold increase was not accepted, Tonan Seiki did succeed in substantially increasing its unit prices. As if following suit, other companies also accepted price increases, and one year after Watanabe was appointed as president, the company's business performance was undergoing a V-shaped recovery. Meanwhile, it strove to improve and accumulate its technologies and expertise with the aim of becoming a company that would survive. Its workload declined significantly in the financial crisis, but fortunately it was able to sell a broad stretch of land it had been keeping as a plant site, allowing it to get through the financial crisis without having to let a single employee go.

Despite being an SME, Tonan Seiki is a 24-hour a day operation, running day and night. As a result of this it adopts a framework that "allows us to do three times the work in a small plant." Initially the Labor Standards Inspection Office did not approve of the company's four-days-on/two-days-off work roster, but came to accept that the work conformed to eight-hour working days and two days off a week. The process management can be carried out by the plant chief at home on a computer, and sales reps undertake their sales activities while keeping an eye on the work schedule, which has also made it possible to eliminate waste. "We got on track by transforming into a company that focuses on large components five or six years ago. Recently I've been able to feel a bit confident about the future," explains President Watanabe. Without a doubt, from here forward also Tonan Seiki will continue to take on the world as a company that performs precise machining work on a large scale, work that no other companies can do.

Aiming to be global niche leader by transforming sales structure

SIGMA CORPORATION is an automobile components maker based in Kure City, Hiroshima Prefecture. It is capitalized at 45 million yen, has a workforce of 200 employees, and generates annual sales of 4.6 billion yen. A joint venture it set up in China has expanded to reach an annual turnover of 2 billion yen. It also established local subsidiaries in Thailand and India. The Thai unit commenced operations at the end of 2014 and the Indian unit will begin in 2016, and the company is hurrying to establish a global supply structure based in Japan. Meanwhile, with automotive components technology as a foundation, it succeeded in making laser light flaw inspection devices commercially viable. The devices make it possible to inspect the inner and outer walls of cylindrical machinery and other devices nondestructively and without contact, and the company has been recognized by METI as a Global Niche Top Company.

Sigma also advanced into segments such as a business in the security field. It is in the process of pursuing a business strategy to grow rapidly into a company with annual turnover of 10 billion yen by 2020.

According to President Toshitaka Shitanaka, "When I took over as president, Mazda accounted for almost 100% of our work. Rather than reducing Mazda's work, I have been making an effort to transform our sales structure to ensure too much emphasis is not placed on a single company." This business policy is getting results, and Mazda-related work now accounts for only 40% of all its work. Areas that have grown substantially instead include industrial machinery components, security and laser-related devices. President Shitanaka has successfully converted Sigma from a Mazda affiliate into an independent company.

At the same time, it is aiming to become a global niche leader in automobile components. The automobile components that the company makes include inflator components for airbags, engine parts, and items for wiper systems. In all cases they are important components of automobiles, but Sigma manufactures the components that are built into products, a niche field that means its products go unnoticed by many.

It mass produces metal parts that use metal as raw material, and resin parts. The metal parts consist of molded finished goods such as shafts and gears, while the resin components are produced by taking engineering plastic as a base material and mixing it with 30-40% glass fiber. Engineering plastic boasts strength that rivals the metals developed for use in automobiles, industrial machinery, aircraft and other machines, as well as the capabilities of plastics, which clearly surpass metals in terms of their workability. Furthermore, Sigma is notable for handling a range of molded parts that are also diverse in terms of their materials, including parts that combine metal and plastic.

Parts makers in niche fields face severe pressure from Japanese automakers on both the cost and precision fronts when it comes to their parts, so they all strive to reduce costs not just in one yen increments, but even in increments of 1/100 of a yen. Single micron accuracy is demanded, and amid that Sigma is notable compared to other parts makers for the production machinery it built in-house using its own technologies, and for successfully realizing substantial cost reductions and performance advancements.

Conventionally, the process for manufacturing wiper shafts involved machining the metal, and then polishing the outer diameter by machine in order to improve the precision, but Sigma developed a new technology for making the shafts using composite technologies such as forging, and a molding process. By eliminating work that caused costs to climb, such as the polishing of the outer diameter, Sigma succeeded in substantially reducing costs. The shafts are by no means inferior to conventional shafts on the performance front either. Thanks to a large automaker adopting the shafts, currently they are being utilized by various domestic automakers.

Resin parts for water pumps are used in engine cooling systems. Sigma proposed to automakers that by making full use of the component processing technologies and expertise it had accumulated, it would even be possible to make the water pump impellers out of resin, and automakers have begun using them as a result. The resin impellers are processed into a three-dimensional shape and improve the pump efficiency by 10%. From around 2000 they began being used in mainstream automobiles as well, not just high-end models. The company developed similar parts also, and currently they are being employed even in light automobiles. Sigma believes it has already secured a market share of over 30%, and because further improvements in fuel economy will be required following the revision of the automobile fuel economy standards from 2015, Sigma is forecasting its share will expand to 70% toward 2015/2016. In 2008, the year of development, Sigma delivered 60,000 units, but that figure climbed steeply to 200,000 units in 2011 and then 5.5 million units in 2013, so the forecast is sure to be achieved.

Parts will be used in 30% of automobiles produced worldwide

An advanced molding machine that Sigma developed itself in 2012 made it possible for one unit to perform all the tasks from delivering the raw materials to molding and punching. This enabled a substantial reduction in the employees needed for the work. Conventional machines could make four products simultaneously in one manufacturing round, but this was taking 56 seconds. The new machine makes products one at a time, but significantly reduces the time needed. Consequently Sigma was able to boost work efficiency by 50%. The weight of the metal molds required was also lightened to one-tenth, from 500 kilos to 50. That alone led to large cost savings, but the area that the machine was particularly effective was the yield (the ratio of product production as a component of the raw material), which Sigma increased to 94%, from 70% previously.

On the shop-floor, work takes place like a procession of robots, and the company is also attempting to automate inspections. Sigma has set a target of achieving a 24-hour, 365-day-a-year unmanned production line. It is steadily achieving results with the goal of leading the world in developing highly efficient dedicated machines and facilities, developing unique robotic technologies and robots, and automating inspections. The company is proceeding to build a network that links five countries worldwide in order to secure a 30% share of the global market in the niche field of wiper components.

As mentioned earlier, the China plant is enjoying success, and many of the products made there are sold to the North American and European markets, not just within China. In addition to China, it has plants in Thailand and India and is currently pursuing plans for one in Indonesia. Once this production network is completed, Sigma will be able to export even greater quantities of products that utilize the company's technologies from its overseas production bases in China, India and elsewhere to North America and Europe. Its sales expansion in the global market will continue as a result.

According to Sigma's calculations, 85 million automobiles will be produced worldwide in 2013. 11 million of those automobiles will use the company's products, a share of 12.9%. Furthermore, 89 million automobiles will be produced in 2016, and 20 million of them will use Sigma's parts, giving it a 22.5% share of the market. 92 million automobiles will be produced in 2017, and 27.5 million of them will use Sigma's parts, taking its share to 30%, the company says.

Advancing into the security field, where customers' needs are becoming diverse

On the basis of the technologies it had accumulated thus far, Sigma embarked on developing businesses in two new fields. One is security. Many products sold at mass retailers and other outlets are equipped with security tags. This is a shoplifting-prevention system that prevents theft by having the tag trigger an alarm if someone tries to exit a store without paying. Sigma is making serious inroads in this field also, and has already established a sales network. It has brought security products to market in areas such as shoplifting prevention security gates, high resolution surveillance cameras, and contactless information identification as an alternative to barcodes. It also sells original tags for security gates. These products apply the high-frequency circuit technologies used in Sigma's automobile parts manufacturing processes. In the past, many security goods were developing overseas and imported to Japan, and so in some cases their designs felt strange to Japanese people. Sigma plans to respond to customers' needs by refining designs and aligning them to the Japanese market, including how the tags are attached to products.

As an example, high-end fashion stores dislike security tags because they undermine the sense of luxury. The same goes for stores that sell high-end handbags, bags for business people, and shoes. Small tags are also required for eyewear and hearing aids. Sigma has developed fashionable and miniature tags in response to these customers' needs, and as a result, fashion company Shimamura, as well as Bic Camera, Akachan Honpo and major used fishing goods chain Tackle Berry now all use Sigma's security tags.

Coincidence and challenge

The biggest factor behind Sigma being selected by METI as a Global Niche Top Company was its successful commercialization of laser light flaw inspection devices. The laser light flaw inspection device initially scans the entire surface of the object to be inspected by irradiating it with laser light. The principle involves exploiting the fact that the angle of light generated from flaws or defects differs considerably compared to direct light and diffracted light. By separating and inputting the respective amounts of reflected light and using a unique technology to analyze changes in them, it thus becomes possible to automatically detect flaws, cracks and other defects. The device's most notable characteristics are that it does not come into contact with the item it is inspecting, and furthermore, it is non-destructive. It has also made it possible to determine whether or not there are defects inside holes in machinery, something not achievable conventionally using visual inspections. Additionally, the inspection data can be retained as defect information, making it possible to feed the data back to the manufacturing front line and significantly reducing occurrences of defective products.

At the inspection area highly experienced employees still carry out visual inspections that rely on eyes and intuition alone. In a visual inspection it is possible to easily distinguish between what anyone can tell is a good product and conversely what anyone can tell is a defective product. However, identifying whether a product is so defective it really cannot be shipped, or whether it in fact can be, is extremely difficult. These troublesome products are sorted out based on the individual inspector's intuition alone. Consequently, in some cases sound products are judged to be defective and defective products are judged to be sound. Shipping unsound products damages a company's credibility, and conversely, concluding that sound products are defective causes costs to rise. Furthermore, the occurrence rate for errors arising from visual inspections increases as the time the inspector spends working passes. The work environment, degree of proficiency, and how the inspector is feeling are also behind judgement errors. The laser light flaw inspection device is thus considered to be a ground-breaking product that has made it possible to carry out inspections using numerical measurements based on scientific data, not just by experience and intuition alone as has been the case up to now.

The development of this laser light flaw inspection device began in 2000 in a joint development with the National Institute of Advanced Industrial Science and Technology (AIST; Kure City, Hiroshima Prefecture). In 2001, thanks to a Hiroshima

Prefecture grant for supporting product commercialization by venture companies, the inspection device was completed. When Sigma developed an automatic inspection device for outer diameter surfaces the following year, it similarly succeeded with the development by using external technologies and capital. "Although our company's technologies were put to use in the security business, there was a considerable element of coincidence to it. But the laser light flaw inspection device is an original product. It was developed as a unique product from the outset," explains President Shitanaka. Taking up the challenge of a new technology through joint research with a public research institution led to the development of a product that represents a complete break with convention.

Although many industry participants acknowledge that the laser light flaw inspection device is a highly outstanding product, so far it has not been cultivated into a product that contributes significantly to the company's sales. However, as the distribution agent, Mitsubishi Corporation Technos, Mitsubishi Corp.'s machinery sector trading company, has begun marketing the product in earnest overseas. Mitsubishi Corporation Technos is a subsidiary of Mitsubishi, the representative major Japanese general trading company. It is a trading company specializing in handling machine tools, industrial machinery, inspection and measuring machines and other equipment. Labor costs are rising steeply even in developing countries whose economies enjoyed ongoing growth thanks to cheap labor, and labor-saving efforts are progressing. Concurrently, the countries are also being called on to make more sophisticated products, and so it was decided to market Sigma's laser light flaw inspection device through an overseas sales network. For the time being Japanese companies are the main customers, but by advancing into overseas markets sales can be expected to grow.

The company was originally set up by the current president's grandfather as Shitanaka Machine Tool Co., Ltd., a subcontractor for a naval shipyard. Because the Japanese navy itself disappeared, the second president, the current president's father, painstakingly transformed the company into a parts subcontractor for Mazda. Nurturing that subcontractor into a blue-chip company that was selected by METI as a Global Niche Top Company was a feat achieved by the current president, Toshitaka Shitanaka. Toshitaka joined the company upon graduating from Meiji University. During his "apprenticeship" for the role of president, his father passed away at 60, and so he took over as president at the young age of 33. Initially he had many doubts, but from 1990 to 1995 he set a target "of transforming into a conglomerate in the future," and changed the company name to the current Sigma.

The conglomerate approach involved proposing ideas for improving even small parts and coming up with one-of-a-kind products that other companies cannot imitate by doing that repeatedly, and products unique to Sigma by establishing world-first technologies. This strategy proved successful with the advance into the security products field, and thanks to that success Sigma's employees also grew more confident. At the same time, it also aimed to become the world leader in precision components such as automobile parts, and strove to make its technologies more sophisticated. This led to it obtaining new proposals for practical applications for automobile wipers and recognition from Mazda as a quality manufacturer, creating a diversified base that included the establishment of the plastic molding operation. From 2001 it then set a goal of becoming a "Creative Futuristic Company," which has produced results in the form of setting up a facility for laser light flaw inspection devices, winning a technology innovation award from the Japan Society of Mechanical Engineers' Chugoku-Shikoku Branch, and being selected by METI as one of "300 healthy small and medium sized manufacturers" as well as a Global Niche Top Company.

The company is not resting on its laurels, however. It is currently in the process of striving to "grow into to a people-based company in the future," and aiming for sales of 10 billion yen and an ordinary profit of 1 billion yen by 2020.

References

(in no particular order)

Arisawa, Hiromi 有沢広巳. Ed. *Showa keizaishi* 昭和経済史. Nikkei, 1976.

White Paper on Small and Medium Enterprises in Japan, 2010 (and each subsequent edition thereafter). The Small and Medium Enterprise Agency.

Trade Statistics of Japan. Ministry of Finance.

Census of Manufacture. Ministry of Economy, Trade and Industry.

Arisawa, Hiromi 有沢広巳. Ed. *Nihon sangyoshi 1* 日本産業史1. Nikkei, 1994.

White Paper on Manufacturing Industries (Monodzukuri). Ministry of Economy, Trade and Industry, Ministry of Education, Culture, Sports, Science and Technology, Ministry of Health, Labour and Welfare, 2010 (and each subsequent edition thereafter).

Mitsuhashi, Tadahiro 三橋規宏, Uchida, Shigeo 内田茂男 and Ikeda, Yoshiki 池田吉紀. Ed. *Zeminaru Nihon keizai nyumon* ゼミナール日本経済入門. 25th edition. Nikkei Publishing, 2012.

The official websites of companies and organizations appearing in this book were referenced to accordingly.

Chapter 1

JFC Chusho kigyo dayori JFC 中小企業だより, vol.10. Japan Finance Corporation Small and Medium Enterprise Unit, Feb. 2012.

MiT. SMBC Consulting, Apr. 2012.

Anshin Life あんしんLife, Anshin-Zaidan.

Tsubamesanjo iimonomeguri 燕三条いいものめぐり. Tsubamesanjo Brand Promotion Office, Tsubamesanjo Regional Industries Promotion Center.

Jidai no kaze o kanjinagara 時代の風を感じながら. Yanagiya Machinery Co., Ltd.

Yanagiya News Willow. Yanagiya Machinery Co., Ltd.

"Nihon hinshitsu shoreisho eno michi" 日本品質奨励賞への道. *Quality Management.* Union of Japanese Scientists and Engineers, 2012.

Kimura, Satoru 木村悟. *Inbe Jindai no gijutsu no densho* 忌部神代の技術の伝承. AWA SPINDLE CO., LTD.

Noda, Yasuyoshi 野田泰義. "Mai wei" マイウェイ *Chubu keizai shimbun* 中部経済新聞. The Mid-Japan Economist.

KBC TIMES, vol. 87. OKB Research Institute.

THE KANAGATA SHINBUN. Kanagata Shinbun, Jan. 10, 2012.

Kita, Hiroshi 喜多弘 and Yasuo Yuasa 湯浅安夫. Ed. *Oe no densetsu* 麻植の伝説. Nobu Insatsusho, 1999.

Chapter 2

Sakamoto, Koji 坂本光司. *Nihon de ichiban taisetsunishitai kaisha 4* 日本でいちばん大切にしたい会社4. ASA Publishing, 2013.

Murakami, Ryu 村上龍. TV Tokyo. Ed. *Kanburia kyu-den: Ryu Murakami x ekonomisuto, shacho no kingen 2* カンブリア宮殿 村上龍×経済人 社長の金言2. Nikkei Publishing, 2013.

Rinen to keiei 理念と経営. Cosmo Educational Book, Mar. 2013.

Keieisha no shiki 経営者の四季. TKC Shuppan, Dec. 2013.

Nihon koko soken repo-to 日本公庫総研レポート, no. 2012-7. Japan Finance Corporation Research Institute, Feb. 20, 2013.

New Top Leader, no. 48. NJ Publishing Sales, Sep. 2013.

Kankyo to bunmei 環境と文明. Japan Association of Environment and Society for the 21st Century, Apr. 2014.

A-gasu 21 アーガス21. Tokyo Metropolitan Small and Medium Enterprise Support Center, Jun. 2013.

Kansai no yuryo kikai me-ka- 70 sha 関西の優良機械メーカー70社. Nikkan Kogyo Shimbun, 2008.

Bplatz press, vol. 142. Osaka Urban Industry Promotion Center, Nov. 2012.

Fole. Mizuho Research Institute, Jan. 2009.

ASAP, no. 4. Techno Management Research Institute, 2010.

Kimata, Hiroo 木股博夫. Ed. *Seijuku shijo o ikinuku chumoku kigyo 100 sha* 成熟市場を生き抜く注目企業100社. PHP Institute, 2008.

SQUET. Mitsubishi UFJ Research and Consulting, Mar. 2014.

Okayama sangyo joho おかやま産業情報. Okayama Prefecture Industrial Promotion Foundation, Spring 2014.

Yasuda, Yukihiko 安田之彦. "Ichiryu ni furetemite" 一流に触れてみて. *Seisanzai (Production Equipment) Marketing*. 生産財マーケティング News Digest Publishing.

Chapter 3

JFC Chusho kigyo dayori JFC 中小企業だより, vol. 2. Japan Finance Corporation Small and Medium Enterprise Unit, Aug. 2009.

JFC Chusho kigyo dayori JFC 中小企業だより, vol. 5. Japan Finance Corporation Small and Medium Enterprise Unit, Aug. 2010.

"Monozukuri genba hatsu" ものづくり現場発. *Nikkei sangyo shimbun*. Nikkei, Nov. 11, 2011.

Kaze no kenkyu 風の研究. Kitano Seiki Co., Ltd.

Sakamoto, Koji 坂本光司. *Nihon de ichiban taisetsunishitai kaisha 2* 日本でいちばん大切にしたい会社2. ASA Publishing, 2004.

Shinoda, Itaru 篠田達. *RF no chi* アールエフの知. President, 2004.

Risona-re りそなーれ. Resona Research Institute, Oct. 2012.

Puresu gijutsu プレス技術, Nikkan Kogyo Shimbun, Oct. 2006.

Authentic Report, no. 19. Seibu Shinkin Bank, 2010.

Nihon koko soken repo-to 日本公庫総研レポート, no. 2013-5. Japan Finance Corporation Research Institute, Jul. 10, 2013.

Kachinokori no Chie Project Team 「勝ち残りの知恵」プロジェクトチーム. Ed. *Kachinokori no chie* 勝ち残りの知恵. Research Institute of Economy, Trade and Industry, 2006.

Chusho, bencha-kigyo to sangaku renkei ni kansuru chosa kenkyu 中小・ベンチャー企業と産学連携に関する調査研究. Organization for Small & Medium Enterprises and Regional Innovation, Mar. 2008.

Hosoya, Yuji 細谷祐二. *Guro-baru nitchi toppu kigyo ron* グローバル・ニッチトップ企業論. Hakuto-Shobo Publishing, 2014.

Chapter 4

Higuchi, Haruhiko 樋口晴彦. *Soshiki no shippai gaku* 組織の失敗学. Japan Industrial Safety & Health Association, 2012.

T. G. Press. Tokyo Guarantee, 2013 Fall.

New Top Leader, no. 30. NJ Publishing Sales, Mar. 2012.

Shoko Journal. The Shoko Chukin Bank Institute of Commerce, Industry & Economics, Nov. 2012.

Nikkei Business. Nikkei Business Publications, Apr. 5, 2004.

Nikkei Business. Nikkei Business Publications, Aug. 25, 2008.

Nikkei Business. Nikkei Business Publications, Mar. 9, 2009.

JFC Chusho kigyo dayori JFC 中小企業だより, vol.13. Japan Finance Corporation Small and Medium Enterprise Unit, Sep. 2013.

TECHNOLOGY. Hachinohe Regional Advance Technology Promotion Center Foundation, Dec. 2007.

Newsweek Japan Edition. CCC Media House, Nov. 14, 2007.

Takei, Norio 武井則夫. *Erabareru riyu* 選ばれる理由. Gendai-Shorin Publishers, 2013.

Chapter 5

JIR Joyo sanken NEWS JIR常陽産研NEWS. Joyo Industrial Research Institute, Sep. 2013.

Chusho koko repo-to 中小公庫レポート. Japan Finance Corporation for Small and Medium Enterprise, Jul. 3, 2007.

The Kaisha Shikiho 会社四季報, vol. 2. Toyo Keizai, 2014 Spring.

Hokkoku shimbun 北國新聞, Hokkoku Shimbun, Dec. 27, 2013.

JBIC TODAY, vol. 8. Japan Bank for International Cooperation, Jan. 2011.

Aoi kaze 碧い風, no. 46. The Chugoku Electric Power Company.

PHP Business Review Matsushita Konosuke Juku PHP ビジネスレビュー松下幸之助塾. PHP Institute, Nov./Dec. 2013.

About the Author

Makoto Kurosaki was born in Gunma Prefecture in 1944. During his time working at Jiji Press he was constantly on the business beat, covering institutions like the Japan Business Federation, the Bank of Japan and the Ministry of Finance. He also reported on major business events like the Recruit scandal. Kurosaki headed the Miyazaki and Fukushima bureaus and served as editor-in-chief and commentator. He left Jiji in 2004 and is now a professor at Teikyo University's Faculty of Economics. Kurosaki's many published works include *Sekai o seishita chusho kigyo* [World-Leading Japanese SMEs], Kodansha, and *Kigyoka no joken* [What It Takes to Be an Entrepreneur], Heibonsha.

（英文版）世界に冠たる中小企業
Global Class Japanese SMEs

2017 年 3 月 27 日　第 1 刷発行

著　者　黒崎 誠
訳　者　ラーリ・グリーンバーグ
発行所　一般財団法人出版文化産業振興財団
　　　　〒 101-0051　東京都千代田区神田神保町 3-12-3
　　　　電話　　　　03-5211-7282（代）
　　　　ホームページ　http://www.jpic.or.jp/japanlibrary/

印刷・製本所　大日本印刷株式会社

© 2015 by Makoto Kurosaki
Printed in Japan
ISBN 978-4-916055-81-1